With
regards(

HOUSE BEAUTIFUL
WEEKEND HOMES

HOUSE BEAUTIFUL

WEEKEND HOMES

The Editors of
HOUSE BEAUTIFUL Magazine

JoAnn Barwick, Editor in Chief

Margaret Kennedy, Executive Editor   Mervyn Kaufman, Editorial Director

Betty Boote, Managing Editor

Text by Carol Cooper Garey

HEARST BOOKS

NEW YORK

Library of Congress Catalog Card Number: 89-084147
ISBN: 0-688-09170-9

Printed in Singapore
First Edition
1 2 3 4 5 6 7 8 9 10

Edited by Pamela Thomas
Designed by Larry Kazal

Produced by Smallwood and Stewart,
New York City

INTRODUCTION

Henry James said that to him the loveliest words in the English language were "summer afternoon." I don't think that I stand very far from Mr. James when I say that *my* head fills with the loveliest thoughts when I hear the words "weekend cottage." They are thoughts of family, warmth, tranquility and ease; thoughts of Queen Anne's lace, log fires and thin curtains moving in the breeze, of birdsong, rowboats and picnics.

Weekend houses are centers for innocent pleasures, retreats that soothe us after the pressure of workdays and the abrasions of city life. I think a lot of us would agree that life in the fast lane includes finding the right exit—the one that leads to our cabins, cottages, farmhouses, remodeled barns and beach shacks. No two families are alike, no two getaways are alike, but the yearning for such a refuge is the same, and it's one that I see more and more as I travel the country, keeping my finger on the domestic pulse.

When we put together this anthology of thirty-five of *House Beautiful*'s most wonderful weekend places, we were struck by the rich variety of house styles and living styles. It pleases us enormously to be able to share this collection with the reading-decorating-building-dreaming public because we discovered that each example gained in stature from the company it keeps. The whole, you will see, is greater than the sum of its parts. The chapters illuminate each other.

I can picture readers still in the planning stage of weekend life getting a new, clear vision of what they really want. Maybe they will see one house they want to imitate; more likely the book will yield a patchwork of inspirations. I can picture other readers who are well established in weekend places suddenly discovering five or ten big or small ways to make them better. I can picture still other readers treating this book as a month-in-the-country sort of armchair tour.

One of the reasons weekend houses make us so happy is that they let us play a role, one that we choose. "This is the real me," we think when we're settled into our Saturday-Sunday routine. In our workaday lives, in cities and bustling suburbs, we have to fit into dress codes and schedules: office schedules, school schedules, train schedules. It is when we go to the country that we play the part we want to play.

One elegant decorator is a country gentleman in the house built long ago by another country gentleman. He displays his grandfather's books in a gracious chintz-

filled living room and keeps his horses in the stable. You can be a country gentleman only on a country estate.

In a ski town in the Far West, the owners of a new house play their chosen roles, as winter-sports athletes living the rugged, healthy life in a lodge. Their log cabin is built with the biggest logs they could find, and the stones for their tall fireplace are boulders. You can taste the after-ski coffee and smell the brilliant clean air when you look at the pictures.

Other weekenders snuggle into a little 1770 smithy on Long Island, enjoying the purity and modesty of those old rooms brightened for today's taste with very un-Colonial white paint. A playful house is not a museum.

Upstate New Yorkers have a pretend-Cotswold ambience in a ten-year-old cottage with steep shake roofs, narrow dormers and casement windows. The handmade house, like its ancient inspiration, has beams cut from a local forest and a hearth made of stone pulled out of a creek on the property. I can imagine ladies dining here in long simple dresses made of muslin, eating bread-and-butter pudding.

The great French couturier Hubert de Givenchy spends his weekends in a *manoir* where the living is opulent yet country-comfortable. There, in bedrooms decorated with linens of his own design, he pampers his guests with every luxury. He loves his role as host.

So does artist Carol Anthony, who owns a tiny blue shed that once housed chickens on her Connecticut property. With a pair of arched windows she had stored for years and a shored-up interior that she whitewashed, the shed is a guest house friends never want to leave.

So many divergent ways to express all the impulses of weekend living—that's what pleases me so much about this book as I leaf through the pages. There's the impulse for hosting and the impulse for solitude. The impulse to rescue a derelict building that just needs a lot of loving attention; the impulse to put a work of architectural distinction into the landscape; the impulse to soak up a sensational view.

No two families alike, no two getaways alike, but all of it wonderful weekend living.

JoAnn Barwick, Editor in Chief
House Beautiful

CHAPTER ONE

COTTAGES

Warm, cozy and ever-so-charming, the cottage evokes images of the countryside or seashore even if it sits on a compact suburban lot. Initially conceived as a laborer's house, the cottage has led a rags-to-riches sort of life. What began as a humble shelter has become one of the most desirable weekend hideaways, a symbol of tranquillity and ease rather than poverty. This passage from *The Country Cottage,* a book written in 1906, is apt today: "The increasing demand for a cottage in the country is not confined to any one class of people, nor is it any longer significant of a humble mode of life. Its elegance lies in what it fulfills of that simplicity and frugality of life."

What is this architectural style we call cottage? Actually, the varieties are as diverse as the inhabitants. An organic style that tends to evolve with each new generation, "cottage" is more a term of endearment than a specific design. Almost any kind of small, single-family dwelling made of traditional stone or clapboard can be called a cottage. The common denominator is a simple floor plan, typically with three or four rooms downstairs and perhaps a second half or fullstory containing bedrooms. What most rural areas and small towns offer is the traditional gabled cottage with a steeply pitched roof and modest trim.

While some of the most engaging cottages are English and European in origin, cottages are also as American as apple pie. The cottage style is indigenous to all regions of the United States; the fact that so many recall their English counterparts is due to the early American settlers who were influenced by native country architecture, particularly the simple designs of England's southeast. The snug clapboard house so closely associated with New England is a descendant of weatherboarded English cottages. Their horizontal timbers were applied over the old wood to give extra warmth and protection. Cottages of that sort were almost always painted white, a custom that continues today, although the clapboard house painted in soft "Colonial" colors is now an important part of the American vernacular.

The cottage is easily adaptable to many styles of decoration. Restful, free of extravagance and easy to care for, cottages have universal appeal. Whether antique or born yesterday, the little house with quaint dormers, a gabled roof, screened porch and intimate garden epitomizes our notion of the charmed life.

AMERICAN COTSWOLD

Windows (*above*) contribute to the storybook quality of this cottage, what with the many small, leaded panes and deep ledges for flower boxes. As in old European houses with extra-thick walls, the windows are recessed to form nooks for plants or even seats. To fashion splinter-free seats, soft pine was rubbed smooth, then finished with the same homemade stain used on all the woodwork. Decorative in themselves, the windows need no curtains—good news for carefree weekends. A collection of country-ware bowls and pitchers (*opposite*) nests on shelves stained in the same fashion as the windowsills.

Where but in the ancient villages of England or the pages of Grimm would you expect to find such a lyrical cottage? This house happens to be in upstate New York, the product of its builder's distinctive imagination. Barely a decade old, Forest House harks back to the half-timbered dwellings of the English countryside whose timbers came from the surrounding oak trees and whose stone was quarried from the Cotswold hills. Typical of the centuries-old Cotswold cottages, this house was handmade with materials native to its region. All the beams came from a local forest and were cut by Amish craftsmen to retain their natural, irregular forms. The fireplace hearth was built with rugged flagstone from a creek on the property.

An untamed garden (*preceding page*) surrounds the cottage's entrance, which is marked by a primitive fence made from leftover pieces of raw wood. The whimsical-looking roof adds to the fairy-tale appearance of the cottage.

The sunken breakfast room (*top, left*) is bathed in natural light from two windowed walls; at night, light is provided by small spotlights near the ceiling beams. Its table and corner cupboard (*above, right*) were made from old barn wood. The kitchen's wide window ledge (*above, left*) like those in all of the rooms, accommodates displays of stoneware and country objects whose earthy colors add to the mellow nature.

The living room (*opposite, top*) is open to the rest of the first floor so that light streams through the house. An old wood beam stretched across the fireplace creates a mantel—yet another ledge for displaying country pots. The deeply recessed fireplace with its stone hearth needs no screen; its iron tools are from a local blacksmith. A French "grandmother's" chair stands nearby. The dining room (*opposite, bottom*) houses an eighteenth-century carousel reindeer.

Despite its fairy-tale appearance, Forest House offers a wealth of creative ideas to borrow for a renovation or a cosmetic change. Rather than a thatched or slate roof characteristic of the Cotswolds, this steeply pitched roof is composed of a random arrangement of weathered shingles. The rough stucco walls give the illusion of age, yet are forever sturdy and clean looking, with only an occasional whitewashing necessary.

To achieve this character of aged stucco, sand was stirred into a can of house paint until the desired rough texture resulted. Applied over plasterboard walls with a trowel, the rough paint was then sprayed with water for a plaster-over-stone effect. Once dry, the walls received a base coat of white followed by a mixture of pink, peach and red tones sprayed on. Finally a wash of white was painted on to blend the colors into an overall mellow tone.

The rustic woodwork was stained with a concoction of tobacco juice, ammonia and beer, and topped with two coats of varnish. This kind of pioneer spirit and handiwork give Forest House the authenticity of an old-world cottage at a very young age.

SMALL WONDER

A s with people of a certain age, cottages often have a colorful past. This cottage, for example, dates back to the 1700s, when it was the home of the community sheepherder on the Long Island shore. Apparently, it was also once a smithy (based on the horseshoes and carriage parts unearthed on the property), and more recently, it housed an answering service (evidenced by over 100 phone plugs found by the owners).

Despite its curious pedigree and derelict condition, the owners thought this house showed promise. Challenged by its shortcomings and stimulated by its potential, they embarked on a rescuing project. With architecture as interesting and diminutive as this, the task of renovating became an exercise in creativity.

A brick-paved terrace (*opposite*), in keeping with the cottage's old character, serves to organize the backyard and create a private court. The mixed border of annuals and perennials is both decorative and functional, for it screens out the neighboring house. Striped cotton covers and white lounge pads are as refreshing as the peonies and potted flowers. The large round table (*above*), positioned near the kitchen door, is easily set for weekend entertaining; its lightweight café chairs can be moved about to form conversation areas. The driftwood tone of the table and chairs blends with the house, which was shingled and stained to an appealing greenish putty color. Brunch is served without a tablecloth so the wood texture adds to the rustic flavor.

First of all, the front door—originally positioned in the center of the house—was moved to allow more seating in the living room. Then the interior of the cottage was doused in shades of white to free it from feeling too close for comfort. Bleached from top to bottom, the rooms are reminiscent of sun-baked drift-wood. The driftwood quality of the timbers was achieved through the art of pickling.

The fireplace, with its unique graduated layers of brick, is now viewed in a new light. Painted with three coats of white semi-gloss paint to emphasize its texture, it quickly became compatible with the lightened timbers and woodwork. The fireplace also serves as a space divider between the intimate living room and the dining area, whose bleached woodwork and white-framed windows create an illusion of spaciousness. What was considered cozy in the eighteenth century would be claustrophobic today; therefore, "whitening" old timbers is a frequently used technique to lighten the interior without obliterating the antique character.

In a house of such tiny proportions, "simple is the way to go," says New York decorator Robert K. Lewis, who suggests limiting color to white and natural tones, using minimal window treatments like gauze curtains and refraining from adding "too much stuff."

A small writing table (*below*) fits snugly in one corner. Botanical prints define the space. The dining area (*opposite, top*) is a fine example of well-used space. Flush against the wall, the banquette takes up less space than chairs would and can seat four if necessary. Its cushions are covered in the same putty-colored fabric as the living room sofa, which again creates an illusion of space. The kitchen counter functions as a sideboard to hold food for buffets or to collect dishes. French doors leading to the terrace allow ample light, which has been suffused into a soft glow by floor-length gauze curtains.

The cottage kitchen (*opposite, bottom, left*) shares the fireplace wall with the living room. The primitive wood planks that encase the counter are made of old stair boards—worn paint and all—and give the kitchen a separate identity. A minimal number of open shelves—rather than wall-to-wall cabinetry—hold all the necessities of weekend living. The tall plate rack has a purpose apart from its obvious charm: numerous brackets for collected baskets, pots and plates. The bleached beams are put to good use as supports for track lights as well as for drying herbs.

In the living room (*opposite, bottom, right*), clues to the cottage's previous life appear on and around the fireplace: shears once used to clip lamb's wool decorate the mantel; an antique "lambing" chair, originally on rockers, is softened with thick cushions for modern comfort. The metal sailing ship, formerly mounted on a weather vane, sits on a "coffee table" trunk. Trunks often serve multiple purposes in weekend houses: as tables, extra seats, and when space is at a premium, convenient storage units.

W hite-on-white is the decorating formula for this compact bedroom (*opposite*), where the main attraction is a four-poster. Its frame (and the floor) has been pickled in the same fashion as the living room timbers to make the wood recede but not disappear. White gauze hangs from simple poles on the windows and on the bed posts, giving the tiny room an open, airy feeling. The only wall embellishments are two swing-arm lamps for bedtime reading. The rule of thumb for decorating rooms as small as this is to use just a few pieces of furniture in a large scale.

T he one element of color in this white-saturated bedroom is a hutch (*above*), which still bears its original paint. Step-backed hutches of this sort have played utilitarian roles in dining rooms and country kitchens as storage and display cabinets. However, this one serves as a novel alternative to the conventional bedroom chest of drawers. Its open shelves house a range of found objects, including a tiny trunk as a catchall. The bottom portion can serve as a second-home linen closet, with sachets tucked inside to infuse sheets and towels with fragrance.

COTTAGE-STYLE DECORATING

The quintessential summer cottage should have a white picket fence and simple yet tasteful decoration. This one, an 1830 Greek Revival cottage in Sag Harbor, New York, serves as a role model, its old-fashioned innocence furnished by Laura Ashley, whose English look has found permanence in America. Because such fabrics and wallpapers are widely available, decorating in this style is easily accomplished. The thoughtful merging of old and new gives this cottage particular distinction.

The cottage (*above*) has little ornamentation save an impressive front door, a sign of its nineteenth-century roots.

The kitchen (*opposite*) has a decidedly fresh outlook, with modern windows transforming one wall into a live mural. The absence of panes opens the view completely, and a fanlight heightens the perspective. Space over the old closets was newly utilized by the addition of a salvaged board, as a shelf for a spatterware plate and country buckets. One can eat inside or out, on the rustic table decorated in what remains of its original paint. The butcher-block island is both a work top and storage unit. The kitchen's color comes from natural sources—pots of delphinium from the cottage garden and a stack of nectarines. Green spatterware and country chairs balance the indoor colors with those of the garden.

*T*ulip- and leaf-printed wallpaper and matching balloon shades envelop the dining room (*top*); the pattern was borrowed from a seventeenth-century Italian book cover. Striped seat pads and a rag rug are crisp accompaniments to a collection of blue-and-white porcelain.

A bedroom in the eaves (*center*) boasts an antique fireplace and priceless, original planked floors. The varying angles of the room and the texture of the fireplace wall are emphasized with white. The bed canopy is ingeniously secured to the ceiling with a "sky" of shirred fabric gathered on two parallel rods. The valances are actually balloon shades that can be lowered to make a cocoon of geometric yet soothing prints. Just enough space between window and bedside table allows for an easy chair covered in a matching print.

The mirror-image guest bedroom (*bottom*) received a new identity through decorating. Stripes and a four-poster bed suggest more height than the snug room actually offers. The striped flap on the window can be pinned back or dropped to continue the pattern of the walls. A small checkerboard serves as a bedside table or can be used for fireside games.

The parlor (*opposite*) owes its perpetual glow to yellow-stippled wallpaper aided by sunflowers. Flowers are liberally spread from sofa to curtains to lamp. The room's molding gets a boost from a wallpaper border in a stencil design.

CHEERFUL THIRTIES COTTAGE

An antique hutch (*opposite*) from Maine functions as an extra kitchen cupboard. Evoking Shaker simplicity, it is positioned for convenience near the kitchen and dining room. The top allows for a display of crockery found on weekend outings. All the woodwork, including that of the handmade, diagonal wood storage cabinet, possesses a unified tone. An over-the-door window, formerly a crawl space, is framed to correspond with the dark woods. Its purpose, however, is to bring in light. This is obviously a house where everything has its place and a sense of order prevails.

The brick terrace (*above*) actually serves as another room and is equipped with a rustic picnic table for informal entertaining or for gathering vegetables from the garden. An old table painted white is typical of the simple furnishings that need only a fresh coat of paint to make them endure.

Cottages with gabled roofs and paired, multi-paned windows emerged during the industrialization of America. Such vernacular houses, built between 1870 and 1940 from standard plans, are being reclaimed by a new generation in search of the simple country life, even if it means devoting most weekends to restoration. Young families, in particular, find that this type of cottage suits their need for roots and yet is receptive to change. Adding space and light to the old framework while retaining the original character are the typical goals. The American spirit of reviving the past is exemplified in this Connecticut cottage, whose place in the woods and charm were its strongest attractions.

A work in progress, the cottage has grown with the young owners, who participated in the labor, from stripping window frames to painting the pine floorboards white with a hint of pink. Once drafty, dark and weatherworn, the cottage was treated to new insulation, a cedar-shingled roof and a variety of skylights. Considerably warmer than it was previously, the cottage also has a sunnier disposition year round, owing to the light that enters from above and through new French doors. Stained, rather than painted, woodwork contributes to the feeling of warmth and ensures easy care, features the owners consider all-important now that the hard labor is behind them.

Surrounded by giant oak trees and covered with vines, this cottage (*preceding page*) epitomizes the ideal pastoral retreat. The symmetry of its windows and the sharp lines of the roof complement the traditional, pristine-white framework. Sturdy Adirondack chairs weather the seasons and are in keeping with the plain cottage style.

The living room (*right*) benefited from the removal of an old ceiling. Its structural beams now exposed, the room has a strong, woody texture similar to a log cabin. Furnished with sundry old pieces, both dark wood and light wicker, it has conversation areas centered around the fireplace—the heart of any weekend house. Access to the outside is through French doors, whose style is compatible with the paned windows. A room designed for pure comfort, it has not one but two thickly cushioned sofas, woolen throws for afternoon naps and large rag rugs to warm the natural wood floors.

TASTEFUL SIMPLICITY

Cottages tend to inspire nostalgia and romantic sentiment. Consequently, they attract collectors of memorabilia who would rather unearth old treasures than buy anything brand new. How these possessions are arranged and put into context is purely a matter of personal taste and develops over time—with experimentation and editing. "Tasteful simplicity, not fanciful complexity, is the true character for cottages" is how Andrew Jackson Downing defined the cottage style. A pioneer of the small, inexpensive house in a rural setting, A. J. Downing was an arbiter of nineteenth-century style for Americans in quest of the country life. No doubt he would consider this cottage a fine example of "tasteful simplicity."

Its owners, as resourceful as they are creative, put their stamp on the cottage—located on a small island off Long Island's North Shore—and thus created a style of their own. Gallons of white paint cleansed the board-and-batten structure and much of the old summer furniture inherited with the house. As an example, the dining room's pedestal table was transformed with white lacquer, just one successful attempt to lighten rooms heavy with dark wood.

This classic seaside cottage was once an annex to a nineteenth-century resort hotel. What had been four small upstairs rooms were converted into one large bedroom (*above and opposite*) generous enough to include a lounging area. Several pieces of furniture inherited from the hotel were freshened with white paint and arranged imaginatively.

The three-fold screen, newly covered in flowered wallpaper, brings color to the predominantly white room. Reminiscent of a rose-covered garden trellis, it complements the gaily patterned tablecloth. The casual arrangement of freshly picked flowers is as much a part of the cottage style as the white-painted furniture and unadorned windows. The graphic rug suggests a tiled floor, another

cottage-style detail, and serves to protect the floor as well as provide a soft cushion for bare feet.

Several examples of a fine collection of antique linen are displayed throughout the room. Covering the lounge is a lace tablecloth, which, come winter, is carefully stored away. A few pieces of old embroidery, framed to render them safe from mildew, are hung above a console painted a soft green, a cottage-style color that is once again in vogue.

*T*he dining room (*preceding page, left*) has a porchlike atmosphere with its white beams, wallboards and airiness. A quiet, neutral setting, furnished only with the barest necessities, it maintains the tasteful simplicity of the rest of the house. Antique towels rest on the backs of chairs; a plain pine hutch, found at a flea market, serves as the room's "closet." Underscored with another sisal rug, the white-lacquered pedestal table needs no adornment, except for a chubby head of cabbage straight from the garden, to make it dramatic. The white earthenware is in keeping with the lightened-up style of the entire cottage.

For anyone lucky enough to have such a big screened porch (*preceding page, right*) decorating is a matter of playing up to the architecture. The two-fold screen, resembling doors, does just that. Simple wicker chairs, impervious to the weather, can be moved about or stationed by the turn-of-the-century table whose legs were cut down for its new purpose. Wicker stools, easily found at leisure-furniture stores, provide individual tables for serving drinks and appetizers. Come winter, the furniture is stored indoors with mothballs scattered about to absorb the humidity that is inevitable in a seaside location.

*T*he owner refers to her style of decorating as "spur of the moment," yet the result is anything but disorderly. To wit, the living room (*opposite, top*) plays up a matched pair of windows, in front of which stand twin easy chairs, end tables and lamps. Even the vases and flowers are paired. The framed prints (*opposite, bottom, left*) add to the unified look. Old black-and-white craftmen's drawings are similarly framed and hung with architectural precision. The pedestal table is both distinctive and useful in the well-organized reading place. An overstuffed sofa has window views and is summer-slipcovered in cool muslin to match the chairs. Sisal matting, a requisite for cottage decorating, is a natural and inexpensive choice for weekend cottage floors. Easily maintained, sisal rugs can be placed over a wood floor, as this one is, or layered on top of wall-to-wall carpeting to create a crisp texture.

The screened-in front porch (*opposite, bottom, right*) creates the focal point for this cottage, and is often the central gathering place for family and guests. The distinctive gambrel roof was used almost exclusively on cottages while the long, narrow windows on the second story were designed to echo the doors of the entrance.

French doors leading to the porch (*right*) reflect both the symmetry and the casual ambience of this house.

Like archaeologists, the owners collected furniture parts scattered through the house. A bag of chair remnants turned out to be all the necessary parts for a matched set. Waste not, want not being the philosophy here, another dining room table was cut down to serve as a porch coffee table.

In the words of its owner and designer, Joanne Creveling Lookstein, "My intent was to make the house look as if I lived there forever. The most important thing is to decorate slowly. Make a list of what is going to happen in the house, and plan accordingly. The first rule is that what is there should never come back with you. Don't go away for the weekend with a car full of stuff. After all, it is meant to be a place to relax and entertain."

Four years in the making, this cottage style is a layering of possessions, a liberation of the old and the dusty and, most decidedly, a haven for sentimentalists.

GAMEKEEPER'S COTTAGE

In England, birthplace of the cottage, we find an incomparable specimen. Not that it was always such. In foul condition, without plumbing or electricity, the cottage found a sympathetic new owner. The Londoner, on a foray to pheasant-hunting country, spied what she calls "a broken, tumbling-down thing that *needed* me." Apparently the need was mutual, for she showered the cottage with affection and two years' worth of imaginative labor. Clearly, the results were well worth the trouble.

A typically English hedgerow and garden bench (*above*) harmonize with the 1720 cottage. Newly installed Gothic-style windows and doors converted the house's personality from dour to uplifting. The renovation actually began with the windows designed by the owner, whose taste runs to the fanciful Victorian style.

This eclectic outdoor table setting (*opposite*) suits the English country cottage perfectly. Assorted antique wicker chairs that winter inside and the garden bench provide seating for lunch guests. Like any cottage worth its salt, this one has a profusion of roses within eyeshot.

*T*he drawing room (*top*) defies convention with its riot of unrelated patterns. In the English manner, it appears to have come together over generations. The scope is old-worldly: seventeenth-century Italian oil paintings hang over the draped French sofa; terra-cotta Scottish deerhounds rest on the windowsill.

*B*runch for six (*above*) is set on the friendliest of dining tables, a circle of inlaid wood with straw pads as place mats. Jovial red walls sport prints by John F. Herring, Jr. Gothic Revival chairs mimic the style of the arched windows.

A bed in the eaves (*opposite*) with a canopy and curtains has a certain French ambience. Enveloped in a delicate floral print with a corresponding border, the bed and its fabric unify the room. The remaining furniture is a carefully chosen mélange: a tile-topped Victorian table with a mirror; a curious rattan recliner and a wicker stand that serves as an end table.

CHAPTER TWO

FARMHOUSES

Old farmhouses are an endangered species, steadily vanishing from the American landscape since the mid-1800s when they numbered over two million. Suffering from neglect and often abandonment, farmhouses and their sundry outbuildings are prey to wreckers who see more value in developing the open land than in preserving vintage buildings. Ironically, the aura of the old farm and all the domestic images it conjures up are what people want in a country house these days. The appeal of the plain farmhouse, the soaring barn or even the lowly chicken coop has become increasingly popular, heralding a new back-to-basics movement.

People willing to take on the task of restoring old farm buildings sometimes find the endeavor more demanding than they anticipated. Nevertheless, virtually all feel the results are well worth the labor. One young couple stripped their seemingly hopeless 1780 structure to its bare bones, then fitted it with new insulation and air-conditioning while maintaining the basic integrity and beauty of the house itself. Now they and their heirlooms coexist in a hospitable climate.

One gentrified place in historic Dutchess County, New York, had led a more charmed life, and required only creative decorating rather than surgery to please its new owner. In the end, it proved to be ideal for the city dweller with visions of being a gentleman farmer on weekends. Here, he could leave behind the honking horns for the quacking of ducks. For him, life takes on a different rhythm with friends gathered around the piano and the fragrance of Saturday dinner wafting through the house.

In California's Napa Valley, one new farmhouse evokes earlier styles that had been razed a generation before to make way for the more avant-garde. With its nostalgic staircase and broad porch overlooking fragrant vineyards, it marks a return to our notion of the good old days, yet it has the advantages of contemporary style and convenience.

Architectural critic Lewis Mumford cited the "simple elemental forms of the seventeenth century farm house" as the role model for this style. The "numerous nooks and hiding places dear to children" continue to evoke feelings of what Mumford called "inner snugness and security."

If current trends persist, the endangered farmhouse will not only defy extinction, but may emerge as the happiest of modern retreats.

FORGOTTEN FARMHOUSE

An old farmhouse often needs more resuscitation than most buyers are willing to undertake. This house, circa 1780, was a particularly sad victim of neglect, with crumbling chimneys and a sagging frame. So hopeless was its condition that it sat empty for four years before someone came to the rescue.

Enamored of its scenic location in New York State, a young couple viewed the house in the most positive way. After all, beyond the asbestos siding, boarded-up fireplaces and linoleum-covered floors, it did have the Colonial flavor they were searching for. As it turned out, several surprises made the owners' perseverance pay off; the hidden fireplaces were exceptional, the concealed floors were made of hand-hewn pine. The renovation, an ambitious venture that required stripping the house to its bare bones, restored its best features for at least another hundred years. Furthermore, since the house required such extensive renovation, the owners could add energy-efficient windows and central air-conditioning, creating a hospitable climate for both weekend residents and the European heirlooms they've collected.

Resurrected on its old stone foundation, the farmhouse (*above*) has a fresh exterior with a traditional front porch and a gracious center-hall entrance. The clapboard siding was coated with natural stain, eliminating the need for painting. Not having to paint a wood house every few years makes staining an economical choice.

The entry (*opposite*), an original feature that impressed the potential owners, retains its wide-planked floors, fanlight windows and Colonial paneling, which is painted in a typical early-American green. An ancestral portrait hangs over a boot rack as it might have two centuries ago.

*F*amily possessions dictated the style of the bedroom (*opposite, top*). The regal bed takes center stage, its canopy and quilt related in pattern. Burgundy tones play up the richness of the mahogany bed; the dark color of the chair rail is repeated in the mats of each painting. Originally built without closets, the room now has a wall of them behind the bed.

Another heirloom bed (*opposite, bottom*) is the prominent decoration in a child's room. With one recessed ceiling light focusing on the headboard and natural light from two nearby windows, no lamps are necessary. The European-looking bed, made in Philadelphia circa 1840, is dressed in a plump fashion that guarantees comfort. An Austrian folk-art ornament that might have stood in front of a fireplace sits on the headboard. A patchwork quilt adds to the bed's—and the room's—exuberance.

*W*hen the fireplace was exposed (*above*), the living room's original dignity was restored. Corner cabinets and a chair railing hark back to its Colonial heritage. Painted in a blue-gray tone, the intricately carved woodwork becomes an outstanding feature. Antique paintings, important in their own right, show best against white walls. The room's color is derived from another heirloom—the imposing oriental carpet—although come summer weekends, a bare floor is in order.

*I*n the hallway, a gilded mirror reflects an intriguing juxtaposition of styles (*above*). Plain country bannisters are presided over by an aristocratic angel.

*T*he old farmhouse's true spirit comes alive in this area of the kitchen (*opposite*), where bread was once baked in the fireplace oven. One of the buried treasures exposed during renovation, the fireplace is a reward for work well done. Impoverished no more, the room has a fair share of finery, accented by Austrian paintings, matched lettuce-leaf porcelain and deep-red-painted woodwork. An antique oil lamp and firelight cast a warm glow on the table readied for a traditional tea.

BLENDING THREE BARNS

Help is on the way for many of America's abandoned barns. The rescuers are typically city folk yearning for a piece of land and peace of mind. Decrepit as old barns tend to be, they stir fantasies of square-dance-size rooms and towering ceilings. In this case, fantasies were heightened by the discovery of not one but a cluster of outbuildings. And the rescuers, Raymond and Mariette Himes Gomez, weren't about to let any go to waste. (Incidentally, Mariette is an interior designer and Raymond is an architect.)

Their saga began on a trip through a Long Island fishing village where the sight of abandoned barns, stables and sheds proved irresistible. Undaunted by bowed walls and collapsing roofs, the couple saw the potential for unique, spacious living away from the confined city quarters they share with their two children. Another

The century-old barns and sheds (*above*) retain their integrity. In adapting the original layout to human needs, the owners apportioned communal spaces as well as sequestered rooms, with the center barn as a bridge. The cupola tops the "adult spaces," including an upper bedroom. Children's quarters are in the opposite wing. Occupying another eave (*opposite*) is a second home for birds.

obstacle: originally the buildings didn't happen to be for sale. But the couple persevered, then set about transforming the barns with the intent to preserve the details that had captured their fancy in the first place. The stable's stalls (old doors intact) were given new purpose and modern amenities, and what had once been horse stables became a suite of guest rooms, a laundry, a workshop, a TV area and a potting room. The symbiotic buildings suggest strong family ties with emphasis on individuality.

A bridge connecting the parents' quarters with the children's gives the soaring main room a gallery (*opposite*). Porch railing and structural posts help to organize the space, part of which is devoted to dining. The living area gets its full share of light from solidly glazed French doors, large second-story windows and recessed ceiling spots. Light, too, are the lines of the stick sofas and chairs—old country pieces formerly used in summer lodges. The painting by Peter Plagens injects a shot of vitality into an otherwise quiet room dotted with Americana, including

a steeplelike weather vane (*above, left*). More than a quaint element, the sculptural piece marks the middle ground between living and dining areas, as does the sofa-height table it stands on. A pair of candlestick lamps provides necessary reading light. They are lined up with wall sconces and reinforce the total symmetry. Large potted trees with ivy spilling from the bases add to the balance.

The adjacent kitchen (*above, right*) seems like a cabin unto itself. Built into a corner of the barn, the work area makes optimum use of space with materials both sturdy and handsome. Dark-stained pine cabinets are new renditions of early carpentry work with the same patina as the country table. Open shelves display tableware and a well-organized collection of baskets, all accessible. Staples for weekend meals are stored in the lower cabinets, which are topped with granite counters for modern efficiency

and endurance. The black appliances and tubular chairs are as sleek as the counters. Structural beams also serve to hold work lights, both long fluorescent tubes and recessed spots—important illumination in such a dark-toned area.

One of the seven stalls (*preceding page, left*) is now a potting room, its upper cabinets made from old enamelware and glass knobs. Lower cabinets, stained to match the floor, have room underneath for gardening baskets. Plants can be hosed off in the deep metal sink blessed with natural light.

Another of the stalls (*preceding page, right*) is fitted for weekend guests with an antique iron bed. The original stall doors offer architectural interest if not total privacy.

The collaboration of architect and designer is evidenced in their bedroom (*above, left*). Working with the shape of the eaves, they created what amounts to a room within a room: the central unit separating the sleeping area and enclosing the bathroom. The headboard is a repetition of the pitched rooflines. With interior architecture as striking as this, little in the way of decoration was needed, save his-and-her rocking chairs and primitive chests, which serve as end tables. The graphic quilt more than compensates for walls devoid of art.

The bathroom (*above, right*) has an eyebrow window among its assets. A narrow strip of black tile marks the border between roofline and lower walls; white tile encases bathtub and sink, both of which have ample ledge space.

The guest wing (*opposite*) includes separate steps that lead to the children's bedrooms. A country cupboard neatly houses books, all visible from the comfortable seating arrangement.

A GENTLEMAN'S FARM

Gateway to the farm, a mighty stone wall and lyrical arch (*above*) indicate a house of substance. The gate, however, is utterly friendly.

Called the library, this room (*opposite*) actually has no books. "I think it's the effect of the wall color," says Grimaldi of the glossy green that does suggest a cozy reading corner. "Guests love to be in this room, especially in winter," he explains. As for the grand piano, "It symbolizes conviviality, and its extravagant form adds grace and movement." Seated on the chintz-covered Victorian chair or on the striped sofa, guests view not only piano but fireplace.

Glen-Duxbury Farm (*overleaf*) includes a "good Georgian house," a pond and a classic red barn.

If you grow up riding horses and then mold a career based on interior design, chances are you will gravitate to the country—that is, if you find a place compatible with horses, chintz, and by the way, chickens and waterfowl. Ron Grimaldi, a New York interior designer, set out to find such a place. Two years in the searching, he raised his expectations to include an authentic Colonial house with pond, please. He got it all: an eleven-acre spread in Dutchess County, New York, that had belonged to a gentleman farmer much like himself.

"A good Georgian house with proper proportions, squarish rooms and high ceilings" is Grimaldi's description of Glen-Duxbury Farm. "Patrician but not pretentious," he goes on to say about his rooms, six of which have fireplaces to warm a steady flow of weekend guests. Every room, in fact, is as convivial as the host himself. A weekend here has all the ambience of a luxurious country inn, stylishly decorated and combined with a bit of playfulness to put guests at ease.

The dining room (*above*) expresses the owner's gregarious nature as well as the playful license he takes with decorating. No less than twelve chairs—eighteenth-century Queen Anne mahogany—are available for weekend dining. The gate-leg table once belonged to decorator Richard Lowell Neas, who turned its top into "marble" with his painterly hand. Grimaldi likes the glow that comes from a ceiling covered in semi-gloss paint over an imperfect surface. Rather than a predictable brass chandelier, Grimaldi hung a German one of the carved wood that, as far as he's concerned, suits the country.

The so-called white living room (*opposite*) boasts a generous display of cabbage roses, the trademark of the legendary Rose Cumming, whose decorating firm Grimaldi heads. His collection of majolica, displayed on old pine plate-racks, brings more garden color to the room. A grandfather's library of books lines shelves integrated with the fireplace. Tea can be taken on the roomy ottoman, otherwise known as a *tête-à-tête*.

Weekend guests have this to look forward to: tiles ornamenting a mantel (*top*) and an assortment of late-Victorian English vases, "junk made by the millions," says Grimaldi, who buys them by the masses. The flower-laden room (*bottom*) is the owner's way of pampering his guests. "Comfort comes first," he says. "I always provide a big armchair, a wonderful bed, beautiful linens." Guests also have a choice of down- or synthetic-filled pillows.

The most elaborate of the four bedrooms (*opposite*) has a Louis XVI barometer hanging over a nineteenth-century marble-topped table. English Regency black-lacquer beds wear chestnut-leaf fabric, repeated in fanciful form on the windows. The walls sport a bandbox striped paper, "a crisp complement to floral patterns," according to Grimaldi.

FARMHOUSE MODERN

Nineteenth-century rural American architecture that took its inspiration from simple cottages and farmhouses came to be known as the Shingle Style. These vernacular houses weathered many a summer by the sea, where they were typically built as family retreats. Their spreading roofs and wide porches continue to inspire new interpretations distinguished by romantic carpentry details such as columns, lattice and gridwork.

This country house, set in a Long Island potato field, is an imaginative variation of the Shingle Style: 2,300 square feet of mostly open space, with a porch and terrace available for expanding weekend activities. The antidote to city living, it is one family's escape from apartment fever.

Architect Jonathan Foster produced a layout comprised of eight rooms with an abundance of breathing space and natural light. Great importance was given to the stairway, an evocation of summer houses of times past.

The open living and dining plan (*above*) is approached through a step-down entry with classical columns adding a formal note to an otherwise casual house. Plain wood floors are left essentially bare for an easily maintained sweep of space. Linking the two levels is an ingenious sofa whose back is also a partition, while its companion is an unexpected stick-style love seat. Color is judiciously used so as not to interrupt the clean flow. Smoked-glass cabinets are the modern answer to the country cupboards of old shingle houses, and the rustic

piece is an actual remnant from an early farmhouse kitchen. With its grand proportions, the staircase (*opposite*) has warm associations with the past, while the simple grid balustrade remains decidedly modern. The landing allows an uninterrupted view of the living area and a closer look at an aquatic painting by Richard Saba.

*T*he library (*top*) is an oasis ascended from the second landing. Its view is a "a constant reminder that one has stepped out of the bustle of urban life into a more soothing world," says architect Jonathan Foster. His version of the poignant window seat captures a different angle of the view across fields to the ocean. Chintz slipcovers and a plush sofa hark back to old sun rooms. A small country table serves as library desk.

Looking out to the landing (*bottom*), another vista and source of light are evident.

The house's widespread roof (*opposite, top*) suggests a cheerful, sociable place. The house is a sturdy presence whose shingles, like those of the earlier seaside house, blend with the roof. A curvy brick terrace (*opposite, bottom, left*) just outside the main bedroom faces southwest to catch the late-morning sun. An array of potted geraniums creates an easy-to-maintain garden border. Afternoon shade can be enjoyed on the north porch (*opposite bottom, right*), which is reminiscent of an old-fashioned veranda. The wicker table and branch furniture are from another, earlier, era by the beautiful sea.

VINTAGE NAPA

Asecond house should provide a playfulness that acts as counterpoint to the workaday life," says architect William Turnbull, whose clients subscribed to the same theory. Hence this delightful interpretation of an ancestral farmhouse, solidly planted in the Napa Valley, land of good spirits.

Before the vineyards carpeted this part of California, these valleys were planted with prunes and dotted with commodious farmhouses. Spreading roofs and wraparound porches blended with the terrain. However, those familiar sights have dwindled in recent years. In the

This farmhouse (*opposite*) seems to be all porch. In fact, the porch measures more than 2,000 square feet, which makes it almost as big as the house itself. It features traditional details such as lattice trim, white wicker and French doors. The widespread roof (*above*) shades the porch and adds strength to the architecture with umbrella-like spokes of natural-wood beams. One rugged pillar is an impressive member of the support system. The all-white deck bonds naturally with the house.

*T*he living room's exposed beams (*opposite, top*) are an important part of the architectural theme, continuing as they do on the porch overhang. While this room could easily have accepted modern furniture, it is decorated in a more traditional manner, with exuberant chintz armchairs and paired classic sofas. The stone-topped coffee table is large enough to serve all the seats.

The view of the bridge (*opposite, bottom, left*) takes in all of the living room and its outdoor scenery. The underside of the bridge turned out to be a convenient surface for mounting lights. The consistent use of white doors helped lighten up this room so rich with paneling.

Farmhouse-style permeates the dining room (*opposite, bottom, right*). The beams, which also house spotlights, are decorated with whimsical stencils. The country cupboard, in tone similar to the woodwork, is considerably older, as is the table, whose original home was a heavy-duty farm kitchen. Accented with shades of green, the room features leaves in abundance in a collection of china, on a ficus tree, and on the roses. Green tints the glasses and colors the ladderback chairs, which are far more spirited now than in their natural wood tone.

Coffered ceilings (*right*) in the double-height living room are stained a golden-honey color similar to the wooden staircase and paneled walls, making the warmth all-pervasive—and the upkeep easy. One skylight pierces the roof, sending a shaft of sunlight downward.

Viewed from the adjacent vineyard (*overleaf*), the house evokes California, old and new.

architect's opinion, "the vineyards have transformed the valley into a garden of sea-green grapes, marred by too many look-at-me buildings." Turnbull credits the builders of old farmhouses with common sense in working with the landscape, a quality he emulates with considerable originality. This house could be called an homage to an endangered species, new vernacular architecture that gives its family a sense of roots as well as delight.

Taking In the View

•

Double Identity

•

View from the Veranda

•

New Slant on the Small House

•

Mountain Home

•

In the Western Spirit

CHAPTER THREE

GREAT ESCAPES

Time was, getting away from one's primary residence to a totally different environment demanded a winter's worth of planning for transportation. In the nineteenth century, families depended on railroad and steamship schedules for their annual playtime. Of course, the very rich had their own yachts, but even they were limited to summer excursions. The twentieth century brought the automobile, the airplane and the three-day weekend, and as the world shrank, remote places became not only accessible but desirable. As more women joined the work force, extra income was relegated to the pursuit of pleasure. Hence the second home, together with the opportunity for adventure, indulging in a favorite sport, experiencing a new locale or realizing a fantasy.

Twentieth-century escapists are settlers of a new breed: hard-driving career people for whom long weekends are the best revenge. The weekend home becomes a place to unwind, to commune with nature, to discover other sides of oneself. For those spending their work week in confining city apartments tied to suffocating schedules, the weekend house is a marvelous antidote.

Here are the kinds of houses that change the metabolism, the tempo of daily life. Diverse in geography and architecture, they are as individualistic as fingerprints. Some are new, the visions of owners who invested in land and took their time developing a style. Some are old, the dreams of romantics whose houses are layered with history. What they all have in common is uniqueness. And inspiration.

TAKING IN THE VIEW

A modest cottage in its former life, this house evolved to suit modern taste and yet still embraces its traditional past. Happily, its remarkable site retains the same solitude and commanding view it had fifty years ago. Covered with a thick carpet of wild roses and beach plums, it looks over the Massachusetts coastline and a picturesque fishing village. The major disadvantage of the house—its restricted quarters—was overcome through clever renovation by architects sensitive to the original structure. The result is a seamless blending of old and new, oriented to the outside with a sturdy style that refuses to tire.

The Shingle Style characteristic of older seaside houses has been embellished (*above*) with modern details that smack of tradition: white lattice and an arched projection. The deck (*opposite*) encircles the house but projects over the back like a pulpit for sea worshippers. Clad in cedar shingles, the new deck blends with the original grayed shingles. The maintenance-free floor is made of redwood, which also has taken on a gray tone from its exposure to the salt air, while its hardwood railing is painted white to harmonize with all the strong vertical elements. Terra-cotta pots filled with white petunias offer handsome simplicity, with no intention of competing with the expansive views. When not set for entertaining, the gray iron table and webbed chairs settle into the scenery like pieces of outdoor sculpture.

Opened to the deck, the living room (*above and opposite*) was also heightened by breaking through the attic to the vaulted roof. Its structural beams are a visual asset to the architecture, as are the vertical wallboards and latticed stair railing. These strong elements refer to the exterior and have a similar openness. To allow for the kind of ample storage a neat weekend house deserves, space underneath the stairs was allotted. Latticework doors give the entire staircase an ornamental quality like that of the gabled projection outside.

In order to utilize a windowed corner of the living room for best views, a banquette was built and cushioned in nautical stripes. Backless, so as not to interfere with the deep windows, the banquette has ample pillows for the comfort of a crowd. The opposing sofa, a stretch of curved sections, is equally accommodating. A primitive trunk and coffee table give rich contrast against the whiteness of the double-height room; a dhurri rug and handwoven blanket add contrast, too, with their soft colors against the bold stripes. Southern and western exposures ensure a steady supply of light with the bonus of sunset views from this thoughtfully arranged vantage point.

DOUBLE IDENTITY

With its front to the New England countryside and its back to the sea, this house imposes itself in two distinctly different ways. Its face spells solid tradition, with narrow clapboards and four-over-four-paned windows projecting a proper image to its Yankee neighborhood. Conversely, its back, or private side, is contemporary and expresses the family's love of sailing, the sea and easy, up-to-the-minute living.

The facade represents a dreamlike recollection of New England houses, according to the architect, Bruce Beinfield. Beinfield expressed his romantic notion of the vernacular house by exaggerating slightly its scale and starkness.

The rear of the house projects a decidedly nautical image. In fact, this aft side "operates much as a sailboat does," says the architect. The window system maximizes natural ventilation and allows the family to harness incidental solar energy, much as a sailor uses the elements. Facing the south with a command of windswept waters, the house's view encompasses a swimming pool that is worthy of a luxury liner.

The living room (*above*), viewed from the third-level balcony, reflects a nautical flavor with its azure blue sofas and sculptural fireplace with a brass-trimmed arch and white-tiled hearth. Like the outdoor deck, the wood floor is light in tone, as if bleached by the sun. The ribbon pattern on the rug and the curve of the coffee table soften the room's geometric lines, as do the shapely pots and mandolin near the fireplace.

The entrance to the house (*opposite, top*) is an abstraction of Colonial Style, with nary a shutter in sight. A central pediment, the only ornamentation, is punctuated by a fire-red chimney. For easy outdoor maintenance and a forever-clean appearance, the access is pebbled with a central rock garden. Corral-type fencing establishes boundaries that sharply define the house's public side.

On the water side (*opposite, bottom*), Beinfield included a spiral staircase much like those used on ships, as well as a chimney resembling a smokestack and a "steering" deck with pipe railing.

*T*he hallway (*opposite, top, left*) delineates the entrance and second level by separating them from the open interiors. Light pours in through the front. A pipe railing marks the landing and refers to the back deck.

Another watering hole (*opposite, top, right*) in the form of a whirlpool bath sits inside sliding glass doors just off the pool. Ferns and plants thrive in the greenhouse environment, while the tile-covered floor remains impervious to wet feet. Ceiling spotlights with dimmers produce dramatic illumination for a relaxing soak at the end of an athletic day.

The stairway (*opposite, bottom, right*) spirals gracefully from the pool deck to the atrium-style upper level.

Cantilevered over the pool is a circular deck that opens off the dining room (*opposite, bottom, left*). The deck's framework extends the frame of the house, with cutouts repeating the windows' symmetry. Tubular furniture of weather-resistant polyvinyl mimics the railing. Even the lights relate to the ship imagery; they are actually boat fixtures with metal-framed globes of smoked glass to eliminate glare.

*F*rom this angle the architectural composition of strong lines and soft curves is most dramatic (*above*). The pool, emphatically outlined in white, has its own reflections. Free of any extraneous details, the deck is sparely outfitted. Twin ficus trees add greenery, yet come frost they can be relocated to the whirlpool area to soak up the sun.

VIEW FROM
THE VERANDA

Many an idyllic summer has been spent here on Mackinac Island, an eight-mile-round oasis between Lakes Huron and Michigan. A popular Victorian resort, the island holds onto its history with a fervor. Horse-drawn buggies still parade on the narrow streets, and landmark houses are so beautifully preserved that Mackinac is often referred to as the Williamsburg of the Midwest. Generations of summer dwellers revive the tradition of gracious living by decking out their porches with the same panache that they impart to the interiors of their houses. Heirloom wicker furniture finds its place in the sun, stationed for the best

A traditional place for socializing, the veranda (*opposite*) is dressed for the occasion with floral-cushioned wicker. The vintage pieces each have an air of individuality; crisply white, like the house, the various weaves stand out, particularly against the well-worn floor painted a cool blue-green.

The living room (*above*) brings the same romantic mood indoors.

The old-fashioned reading nook is tucked into a bay window. The skirted table is capped with an embroidered cloth; more handwork is evident in the rosy needlepoint pillow. A brass oil lamp and wicker chair seem fitting in this romantic corner.

The 1876 frame house (*preceding page*) is plainly classic with slender Colonial windows and two dormers. The veranda, a porch of a special kind, is a continuous open space bordered by posts and railing. It also has its own roofline, the underside of which is painted sky blue.

The pink-tinted living room (*above*), like the spacious veranda, is designed for conviviality. Decorator Georgina Fairholme played up the views and tall ceilings with floral-draped windows and jaunty valances. The fireplace's random stones tell of handcrafted masonry; its subtle tones are picked up in the area rug, which helps organize one conversation space. Loosely arranged lilacs and generous bouquets are daily additions to a room that also seems fresh from the garden.

Taking complete advantage of the long room, Fairholme fashioned a second conversation area (*opposite*) with a botanical theme. Three floral prints in oval frames underscore a square painting and accent the love seat and slipper chairs. The needlepoint rug balances the floral arrangement.

views of clipped lawns ready for a game of croquet. The veranda, often stretching across the entire front of the house, is an indispensable room that's decorated for public appreciation.

Inside, the house is no less appealing. Decorator Georgina Fairholme uses fresh, summery colors that preserve the airy quality of the rooms and infuse the house with charm. Reflecting the island's natural beauty, floral prints abound on curtains, cushions and chairs. Unabashedly nostalgic, the floral-strewn patterns and gentle colors recall the old-fashioned gardens cultivated by green thumbs of early Mackinac.

Old tongue-and-groove wainscoting in the bathroom (*top*) made decorating a matter of choosing traditional complements, such as the toile fabric skirting the sink. Mats on the framed shell prints repeat the prevailing aqua tone; the wall decoration takes a Victorian turn with the fanciful mirror sconces. "If you have a little extra space," says Georgina Fairholme, "put a chair in the bathroom." Creature comfort is, after all, the essence of weekend living. A handwoven scatter rug, an old towel rack and decorative pitchers are additional thoughtful touches.

Overnight guests repair to this bedroom (*bottom*), a jovial mix of blue patterns. Old pine beams, left in their original tone, contribute to the warmth. The dado—wood panels that cover the lower walls—has been painted white to blend with the cottage beds and chest. The garlands stenciled on the chest and the scallops painted on the floor enhance the architectural details. They were applied by Kate Williams, an artist who spent childhood summers in one of the island's heirloom cottages. Her scalloped motif is repeated in the wallpaper border and on the edges of the stitched coverlets. The flounced ottoman and dressing table display ingenuity with a few yards of fabric. Delicately patterned curtains, smocked across the top and tied back, frame the tall windows in the simple and softhearted manner of the room.

A trio of old prints (*opposite*) and a vase of fragrant peonies add to the nostalgic composition replete with a guest chest. Salvaged furniture can be rejuvenated with skillful paint techniques.

NEW SLANT ON THE SMALL HOUSE

Rather than restore a well-situated, established house some people opt to start from scratch. That decision presents an opportunity for architectural originality specific to the owner's needs. A case in point is this house, actually three pavilions designed to be energy efficient and easily maintained.

The outdoor-loving owners found a hilly site amid a forest. They also found architects undaunted by their demands: to create tight spaces that could be shut off from one another when children weren't in residence, and to preserve as many trees as possible as they worked. These provisions resulted in an unusual three-part house resembling a series of cabins. With its cedar siding and steeply pitched metal roofs, the house evokes the older houses indigenous to its area of New Hampshire. However, this one-of-a-kind interpretation, compressed into 1,680 square feet of efficiency, represents the height of originality.

This small house (*opposite*) is made of a procession of pavilions beginning with the living area, followed by a bedroom and an enclosed porch. Steeply pitched roofs allow for loft spaces. Screened "spaces'" (*above*) link the pavilions with one another and the woodlands.

*T*he smallest pavilion (*top*) magnifies its corner view. First in the stepped-up sequence, the screened room incorporates the forest with its view and its rustic furnishings, from the natural wood sills to the floor. Both tables have oval glass tops that allow the latticework to show through. Striped upholstery was the logical choice for this tightly organized space.

The middle pavilion (*center*) houses a teenager's sleeping loft above and a study area below. Independently heated with a wood stove piped to the ceiling, the room is also warmed by sun from the skylight and a large loft window. An inset area lined with white tile provides handsome protection from the stove's heat. Steel encircles the pipe for insulation and repeats the pattern of metal tubing used for the ladder rungs and loft railing.

This sleeping area (*bottom*) is secluded in the largest pavilion, above the dining and living rooms. The bed's headboard, in fact, also serves as a space divider and mantel; the pipe leads from a wood stove that is the prime source of heat for this self-contained unit.

A glassed walkway (*opposite*) incorporates the vista and vastly increases the house's modest space. Its natural wood floors and ledges work in harmony and are easily swept clean.

MOUNTAIN HOME

The cabin's chunky texture comes from extra-wide logs and boulder-size stones that form the fireplace (*opposite*). The same hands-on labor went into this cabin as into those of the seventeenth century. The only difference involved small but significant touches of modern finesse. Each log was carved or notched on the underside to make the joining tight, thus leaving no air spaces between them. The economy of building a cabin is in its one-step construction: framing, insulating exterior sheathing, interior sheathing, and finishing are simultaneous. But unlike its forbears, this cabin is heroic in proportion. The furnishings are oversized and extra sturdy. The country pine coffee table is tough enough to act as a leg rest after a day on the slopes. Recreational facilities for this family lodge are a stone's throw away (*above*).

We have the Swedes to thank for the log cabin. During the 1600s, they moved to America's wilderness and brought an expedient construction technique that was to become symbolic of self-reliance. Any man with energy and the most basic carpentry skills could build a log cabin in a fairly short time. The earliest cabins were made with horizontal logs piled on top of each other, with corners notched and fitted to lock the frame. Walls were rendered relatively weathertight with mud or moss packed around the logs. Stones unearthed in the log-clearing process became chimney material. Considering that many of these cabins took only a couple of days to build, their centuries-old endurance record is remarkable.

The log cabin's recent surge in popularity has resulted in new variations on the old theme—with somewhat more ambitious building plans. The rugged individualism we equate with log cabins is found in the ski country around Ketchum, Idaho. Determined to build a house of logs, new-age settlers went in search of raw material. Not that the owners cut down their own trees, but they did hand-pick the biggest logs they could find. The sizes they selected ranged from 19 to 24 inches in diameter, whereas normal-size logs are about 16 inches in diameter. Everything about the house, in fact, is bigger than usual—and to great effect.

*T*he kitchen appliances (*opposite, top*) were designed to endure as long as the cabin; the heavy-duty restaurant range is particularly suited to the hearty appetites of resident athletes. Cooking, baking and grilling all take place under the black steel hood that houses a powerful exhaust fan. Counters are sturdy, too, made from extra-thick, 3½-inch butcher block. Big scale is the nature of this house, down to the extra-wide window and door moldings as well as floor boards.

The dining room (*opposite, bottom*) seems carved out of the forest; its antique hutch blends so well with the walls, it might as well have been made from the same Montana pine trees. The pine hutch is a subtle background for matched plates and a pair of porcelain ducks. The trestle table and chairs are a Belgian carpenter's expression of mountain style using old wood.

Like the kitchen, the dining room has access to the outdoors. With each windowed door comes an additional view—and a break in the heavy pattern of logs. In an environment so dense with wood, light is an essential ingredient. A final note about the log walls: they are untreated inside.

The living room (*above*) matches the outdoors in natural textures. Touches of apricot complement the honey-toned logs and weathered rocks. A large window and French doors open one wall to a vast amount of scenery and light.

IN THE WESTERN SPIRIT

At the foot of the Grand Tetons in Jackson Hole, Wyoming, sits a house that appears to have grown out of the landscape. Its naturalness resulted from the owners' "responsibility to the land." Motivated by respect for the rugged site, they consulted architect Jonathan Foote, whose poetic notions of the American West won them over. So did his resourcefulness. A thrifty sort who recycled cabin logs, barn timbers and native stone, the architect deftly merged the house with "the natural phenomenon of the landscape."

Wide open as the sky, the house satisfies mountain climbers, whether actively engaged in the sport or contemplating. Every room has a generous view, and the entire structure reflects the same directness as the land. There is nothing timid about this house; obviously it has nothing to hide.

The house has been decorated for solid comfort, with an emphasis on big, functional pieces of furniture and rough-hewn textures. Patterns run to the geometric variety, in stripes or ethnic motifs that have the same clarity as the architecture.

A pastoral view from a bedroom terrace (*top*) includes a lacy wrought iron fence and a romantic flower box—European-style details utterly appropriate in the rustic setting.

A passage from the house to the garage (*bottom*) evokes early covered bridges and was actually constructed from recycled timbers. The archway points upward as if continuing the sequence of the rafters.

The entrance (*opposite*) acts as a sun parlor, with solar heat stored in the stone beneath its terra-cotta floor. Every door has a distinction: the closet of crossed planks, the leaded-glass French doors and heavily paneled main door. Twig furniture, an Indian rug and old apothecary chests give visitors their first clues that this is a highly imaginative house, and the ultimate escape from convention.

At the core of this house is a double-height main room (*opposite*) that flows into the dining room and kitchen. A south-facing greenhouse glazes one end of the room, its square windows matching those above. The horizontal seating arrangement and built-in shelves, along with big wood chests, make the taller-than-wide space intimate and self-sufficient. Striped upholstery and rug anchor the open area to a massive stone wall and fireplace where guests are bound to congregate before dinner.

The freestanding staircase (*above*) climbs the house as if it were mountain steps.

One bedroom provides a window seat (*top, left*) or a scenic nook for an extra guest. With a wall of old logs, vaulted ceiling and terrace, it has the feeling of a separate cabin smartly dressed with a spare amount of furnishings that include an antique trough for magazines and a basket for knitting. Another bedroom (*bottom, left*) incorporates a stone wall with a vista. Double doors with solid areas of glass make the most of the glorious view. An armoire functions as the closet, with an old standing mirror as ornament and "dressing room." Both bedrooms have round tables draped with linens, rather than conventional desks, for weekend reading or private dining.

The house's rooflines pay homage to the mountains (*overleaf*); even its areas of white correspond to snow-capped peaks.

The Mill

•

Rustic Schoolhouse

•

Little Blue Shed

•

Chicken-Coop Cottage

CHAPTER FOUR

A HOUSE BY ANY OTHER NAME

"There was an old woman who lived in a shoe," goes the nursery rhyme, and yet by the sound of it the shoe-style house was undoubtedly cramped. However, the idea of living in something other than a conventional house is eternally intriguing. Imagine escaping to a one-room schoolhouse, a converted windmill or a shed that had once been shelter to chickens. In fact, it takes a sense of adventure and more than a dollop of creativity to make a home out of a schoolhouse. What motivates people to make something habitable out of old woodsheds and such? It may be the explorer instinct, a desire to cultivate new territory, and perhaps most importantly, an artistic eye that visualizes the possibilities.

One example is a derelict little shed down the hill from the main house. What would have been firewood to some was imagined by the artist who bought the property as a guest cottage. Her mind's eye converted the sorry place into a lyrical cabin, two walls of which would be transformed by the arched windows she'd found at a salvage company and stored for future use. The windows evoked images of ancient Italy and the classic architecture of Palladio. Incongruous, perhaps, to mention the elegant Palladian style in conjunction with a common shed, but that's where the leap of creativity takes over. Imagine if the old woman in the shoe would have thought to make circular windows of the eyelets!

THE MILL

The window seat (*opposite*), romanticized with book shelves and a backrest, has become one of the more popular retreats in the house. Foam-filled cushions fit the angled seats; pillows are covered with fabric adapted from dish towels. Filmy curtains and pots of geraniums set the stage for a weekend's worth of escapist reading.

The Shingle Style house (*above*) evolved from an old windmill. Croquet is part of the family tradition, as are lawn parties for the clan. The artistic hand at work belongs to a member of the younger generation who's given to setting the table with layers of cloth and a bouquet from the cutting garden.

Weekends can be communal affairs, with aunts, uncles and cousins gathering at the old homestead. Take the case of The Mill near Providence, Rhode Island. Its history goes back to 1812 when it was an octagonal windmill. Subsequently it was converted into a summer house. Five generations have vacationed here since. Family heirlooms are part of its legacy, with one younger descendant usually acting as aesthetic director to make sure old treasures mix comfortably with newer acquisitions.

The parlor and porch (*above*) haven't changed much in the course of time. Floral slipcovers and sheer white curtains are the traditional summer dress in a room that wears its history on its rustic walls.

"Charmed magic casements opening on the foam" is a poetic message carved over the picture window by some ancestor or other. The passageway has another carving in plaster—this is a more obvious homage to the sea.

In the living room (*opposite*), the window seat and its nearby fireplace provide character and focus. As it happened, the paneling came from a house in Providence, Rhode Island. Walls tinted green set off this grand woodwork. Summer comes to the house with unadulterated joy, as flowers everywhere prove. Even the fireplace screen is replaced with a pot of daisies. In the spirit of the season, the floor is covered with a sisal carpet and topped with several thin country rugs.

Most summers the family completes a decorating project, along with their gardening and the usual repairs an old house demands. Recently, the guest bedroom (*opposite*) was treated to candy-striped wallpaper and whitewashed floors. It's a myriad of pastel fabrics and cottage furniture painted to correspond. Originally the bedroom of a great-aunt, this was once somber with dark woodwork. Its odd angles have been made interesting with a striped wallpaper border; prints are hung asymmetrically in character with the room.

A sitting nook (*top, left*) boasts more than a hint of Victoriana. An eccentric wicker bench has a cluster of wallpaper-covered boxes at its feet. Above it is an arrangement of antique plates and prints. The bureau (*top, right*) was a plain chest in its former life. Its handpainted flowers seem to be plucked from the hooked rug. The customary dressing table (*bottom*) with the owner's memorabilia is stationed in front of a window, the ideal location to capture natural light on her face.

RUSTIC SCHOOLHOUSE

One-room schoolhouses have lost their purpose in modern society; however, they've also been known to be salvaged as historic souvenirs, cleaned up and given new identities. Located in Millbrook, New York, this rustic schoolhouse is vintage 1865. Initials on the original wainscoting attest to its pedagogic past, which included a half-century of obsolescence. Architects Mac Clapp and Jimmy Crisp bought a sorry case complete with a rotted belfry tilted like a cockeyed hat. Nevertheless, the structure gave them a rare opportunity to reinvent stylish one-room living. What they devised makes active use of the 800-square-foot space, including sleeping lofts in the rafters. They preserved the outward charm of the original building, but with creative interior design, gave a historic American souvenir new purpose.

Lovingly restored, this nineteenth-century schoolhouse has an elegance born of its neat proportions and simple decorative touches. The single shutters (*above*) are the same width as the front two-over-two windows. Found broken in a nearby toolshed, the shutters contributed to the authenticity of the exterior restoration.

Placed over the living area and kitchen, the sleeping lofts (*opposite*) have narrow balconies that serve conveniently as frames for quilts. The quilt patterns, together with the stenciled designs on the cellar door and chairs, add a folk-art touch to the modern interior architecture, while pine floors and dining furniture subtly complement the overall feel of the plain house. A pie safe in the compact kitchen serves as a decorative variation on ordinary cabinets.

*T*he kitchen pie safe (*opposite*) is positioned under a black iron rail with S-hooks for hanging iron pots. An abstract painting on wood, flat southwestern baskets, white earthenware and a mother-hen tureen create a graphic decorative setting. The living area (*top*) is an educated mix of antiques coupled with reproductions of English, Irish and American descent. A four-panel screen creates a rich backdrop that can be moved to suit mood or necessity.

Pine steps lead up to the loft (*bottom*); simple copper tubing is used as a railing. The croquet set, obviously weathered by many weekends of use on the lawn, adds its own decorative touch.

LITTLE BLUE SHED

The outbuildings that dot the property of many country homes can turn out to be excellent miniature guest quarters brimming with opportunities for imaginative decoration. This tiny space was reincarnated from a rundown shed that once housed chickens. When artist Carol Anthony purchased her Connecticut property, she visualized the shed's transformation using a pair of Palladian windows she had found years before, and went about bartering her artwork in exchange for carpentry. After the windows were installed, the shed assumed a new identity, even exuding a hint of sixteenth-century Italian grandeur. Whitewashed up to its rafters on the inside, painted blue on the outside, the little place became as luminous as a Carol Anthony painting.

New shelves attached to the original planked walls (*above*) appear to float. White objects recede into the background; an Anthony painting and fellow artist's vase command attention.

The poetic-looking shed (*opposite*), with a rocking chair trained on the field, boasts a white Dutch door, one of the carpentry details that make the shed anything but common.

*D*iminutive as the cabin is, it does not feel confining. This is due to the white space that's free of objects and the big perspective from inside (*opposite*). A sense of order and spareness, reminiscent of Shaker houses, prevails. However minimal the furnishings, there is great sentiment in each piece—the drawing table belonged to Anthony's father; the chair came from her childhood home.

*U*nusual wicker chairs (*above*) focus on the view through one of a pair of Palladian windows the artist found years before acquiring the shed. "A magical place" is how guests describe their stays here.

CHICKEN-COOP COTTAGE

*B*rick floors in the sitting room (*opposite*) are repeated throughout the cottage, an aesthetic and practical advantage. The owner notes that the floors are compatible with his many plants as well as his pet chickens and baby geese. Brick, the hardiest of materials, is unsealed and unwaxed. A wall-to-wall collection of Chinese export porcelain is in good company with fine pieces of antique furniture.

*T*he house (*above*) still looks comfortable in its rural context. The former "homeowners" find it a nice place to visit, but not necessarily to stay.

*T*alk about the shrinking of American farms. A century ago, there were 900 acres of rich pastureland belonging to the Rosselli family. Much of the acreage has been sold off, with the remainder being newly cultivated by descendant John Rosselli, an antiques dealer with a keen eye. In a chicken coop he saw potential for guest quarters.

What had been shelter for chickens and doves is now the bedroom of a house that hatched, as it were, from a mere shed into 4,000 square feet of stylish living space. Its former inhabitants live elsewhere on the property and come to visit often. On weekends the owner travels from his New York headquarters to claim his territory.

A dining table designed by the owner is central to this beamed room (*top*). Made of oak, the table has a built-in lazy Susan that revolves an entire meal including wine—all the better for the host, who can enjoy the self-service freedom on weekends. An eighteenth-century pine mirror is juxtaposed with a primitive pitch fork. Beyond the table is an improvised buffet made from a thick wooden plank resting on brick posts.

Off the living room and kitchen is a greenhouse extension (*above*) whose inhabitants include orange and lemon trees, oleanders, camellias, orchids, amaryllis and cyclamens, which flourish in the southeastern exposure. Quilt-patterned pillows are an exuberant match for the flora.

Living up to its romantic image, the cottage is covered with grapevines that create an arbor at the entrance (*opposite*).

All-American Country

•

Imaginative Leap

•

Remaking History

•

New Frontier

•

Modern and Mellow

CHAPTER FIVE

PERSONAL VISIONS

Chasing a dream is reason enough to take you elsewhere on weekends. How the dream comes to fruition has to do with individualism, the special needs and vision of the dreamer.

Locale is a great stimulator of the imagination. The seaside, for instance, sends messages of grayed shingles and sandy decks. The mountains spur images of rugged landscapes and mysterious trails. Streams, rivers, ponds and wandering brooks play their own tune that affects the senses in ways only you can feel.

The sound of water falling so enticed one couple that they devoted every weekend to visiting the site, a Connecticut ridge. After long walks on the property, they'd stop for lunch at a local inn and discuss what kind of house would do the land, the waterfall and themselves justice. This pursuit of a vision made reality of dreams and partners with nature.

Frank Lloyd Wright, who created the landmark modern country house Falling Water, put it this way, "Form derives its structure from nature and from the character of the material and its conditions, exactly as a flower forms itself according to the law which lies in its seed."

The rugged landscape of Wyoming excites another form of self-expression. It is a mountain cabin for modern pioneers determined to get as far away from conventional living as their wheels would take them. Locale: the foot of the Grand Tetons, nirvana for skiers and climbers.

Personal vision isn't necessarily built on a new foundation. It often evolves from the well-worn houses that tug at the heartstrings. It could be the old clapboard and peeling shutters, somewhat askew, that stir the emotions. Or the front porch that brings to mind summer afternoons with iced tea in one hand and a gothic novel in the other.

New or old, modernistic or traditional, these houses have at least two characteristics in common. They are emphatically personal and worlds away from a routine weekday life.

ALL-AMERICAN COUNTRY

*T*he good country life is found on the front porch (*opposite*), where hospitality begins. Pots of geraniums make a garden of the ledge; antique wicker is ever-gracious. The pillars came from a dismantled house.

*P*ine-framed stars and stripes (*top, left*) flank an old painted piece that might have been a stand-up desk in its former life. A craftsman's version of a ram (*top, right*) is carved from tin. Household items (*bottom, left*), include old bread boards displayed in a primitive box that doubles as a picnic hamper. Mary Emmerling (*bottom, right*) stands by her folk-art flag gate.

*F*lea markets have probably furnished more country houses than have furniture stores. In fact, roaming from one fair to another is a favorite sport of rural weekenders. The style with which these regional discoveries are put together is what has come to be known as American Country. And the woman who helped propel the style from coast to coast is Mary Emmerling. As a design professional and an author, she's charted the course of a decorating fashion that began with rooms bulging with baskets, floors covered with rag rugs and walls hung with quilts. Concurrent with the craze for

An antique quilt (*top*) is in concert with a country shelf, nested baskets and a Shaker-style box filled with potpourri. What every country house could use is a pantry (*bottom*) fitted with enough shelves to house everyday tableware and tools. The window wears a towel as a curtain.

The major structural change, enlarging the living room doorway (*opposite, top*), made a dramatic difference. The first floor is basically open with light unobstructed by window coverings other than airy lace fabric. Striped pillows and a checkered rug are successfully paired with chintz, as proven here. The open kitchen (*opposite, bottom*) boasts old wainscoting and a walk-in pantry. The kitchen is free of over-the-counter cabinets; instead it has windows and is wide enough to accommodate a table.

Americana is an increasing awareness of its potential as folk art. Museums and art galleries educate through traveling exhibits; magazines focus on such treasures as antique toys, and auction houses report prices for weather vanes and primitive furniture.

The American Country Style is in another phase of its evolution, an edited-down version with more selectivity and less clutter. Perhaps nouvelle-American Country is a more suitable term for this new approach. So it is with this shingle house on Long Island, pared down in its decorating and geared to summer weekends with a stream of guests.

Once part of a farming community, the house (*top*) has the requisite front porch for watching the goings-on in the neighborhood. City people who come to the village for a weekend taste of country life take special delight in the grace and conviviality of this particular porch.

Entertaining is usually an outdoor event (*bottom*) with the pool as a center of attraction. Heart-shaped goat cheeses are coated with herbs from the garden (*opposite*), a terraced area at the foot of the pool. The wood picnic table, weathered from being outdoors year round, is dressed with layers of homespun cloth appropriately colored for this Fourth of July celebration.

Upstairs bedrooms and an old-fashioned bath were painted all-white to stay with the simplicity of the original farmhouse. However, the owner did indulge in a renovation of her bedroom (*top, left*) by raising its ceiling into the attic. The result is a cathedral ceiling with beams and loft space. The heart motif, a symbol of American Country Style, forms the headboard made of bent hickory twigs.

Another heart (*top, right*) has carved birds perched on it. A delicately colored quilt and corresponding rag rug create a gentle home for a young girl and her bears.

A boy's dormer room (*bottom, left*) has a second bed for weekend sleepovers. Not even the bears digress from the color scheme, which is compatible with any age. The sailboat also has no age limit; it can be considered sculpture.

A basket of rolled towels (*bottom, right*) is a creative storage solution; a wicker table improvises as a sink counter. The white pitcher gets a new bouquet of cosmos each weekend, furnished by the cutting garden. A striped sheet, smocked across the top, decorates a plain sink (with hiding space underneath for supplies).

The old farmer's entry (*opposite*) still serves a utilitarian purpose. Herbs are hung to dry in the natural light and the primitive bench doubles as a window seat and shelf. This floor and all the others were stripped and pickled to create a feeling of lightness throughout the house.

IMAGINATIVE LEAP

Some houses defy labeling. Neither cottage, nor barn, nor farmhouse is singularly apt as a description of this hybrid, which might evoke a country church or perhaps a meeting house on a village green. Elements borrowed from old vernacular buildings have been integrated to create a house with character and appeal. Undeniably charming, it struck the fancy of a couple whose country-house hunting went on for two years and whose criteria were small size and old age. This house qualified as far as size (1,900 square feet) was concerned, but age turned out to be in the eye of the beholder.

Built in the 1980s in Bridgehampton, Long Island, this house conveys the image of a well-preserved antique. And because of its unblemished condition, weekends are essentially maintenance-free.

The entrance (*above*) features Colonial details combined with a majestic arched window. Such emphasis on vertical space enlarges the sense of scale.

Intersecting gables (*opposite*), with the center gable marking the entrance, establish an evocative symmetry. Traditional details like the lattice panels are original touches used instead of predictable windows. Natural light is captured through cleverly placed windows.

Instead of conventional white clapboard, the house is painted a pearl gray with the roof, chimney and driveway pebbles blending in unison. Foundation planting is purposely light so as not to choke the front. Small rhododendrons produce a blaze of color, while more than thirty dogwood trees create an enviable setting each spring.

Snug in the old-fashioned sense of the word, the kitchen (*above*) has more breathing space than normally found in small houses. Extra-wide doorways lead to the dining room, easing the way for food transportation and movement of furniture. Similarly, French doors allow extra light to shine into the woody room, and the terrace becomes an outdoor dining or sitting "room" when weather permits.

Access to the outdoors stretches the living room's borders (*opposite, top*). The windowed doorway capitalizes on floor-to-ceiling space, as does a large window that has a half-curtain of lace with a swag tacked casually across. In a house with limited space, versatility is key. The country trunk, which holds linens, doubles as a coffee table; the Swedish pine sofa can become a guest bed. Extra tableware is stored in the cupboard.

A skylight and a circular window in the eaves (*opposite, bottom*) makes this little bedroom a heavenly spot. With the top half of an arched window at bedside, there's no chance of feeling shut in. Romantic antique linens drape a small round table and are gathered on a window pole in a flounced-skirt fashion.

REMAKING HISTORY

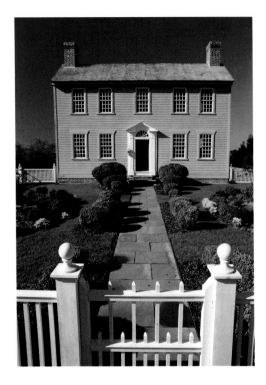

It takes a certain confidence to buy a house from a photograph. And if the actual house is no more than a pile of posts, beams, bricks and moldings stored in two trailer trucks, one must double the confidence and add blind faith.

The fact is, this house, or what amounted to 2,000 parts, was once such a fine example of Federal architecture that it had received National Register status. When the town of Fall River, Massachusetts, couldn't raise enough funds to save the 1789 relic, a call was put into to The Weather Hill Restoration Company. Somewhat

New wiring, plumbing and insulation are the hidden assets in this carefully restored Federal house, whose facade is true to the original (*above*). Its generous number of windows helped sell the dismantled house; each bedroom, for example, has five. Interior shutters (*opposite*) of different designs are part of the house's early architecture. The corner beam is, too. This corner displays the owners' taste in American Country pieces: a bench with vestiges of old paint and a turned-wood chair with homespun fabric and a cloth doll.

like a foster home for houses, the Vermont firm stores dismantled parts until an adoptive family appears.

Enter two partners in a New York antiques business. What their lawyer called a "truckload of sticks" was to become a triumphant restoration in the old house-raising style. Antique tools aided the preservationists, who enlisted a group of friends to participate in the construction, as would have been the way in the eighteenth century. Two customs were revived in the process: nailing a pine tree to the old wood after the raising of the post and beam framework, so that a living spirit could pass into the house, and with the celebration of the completed house, the hanging of a cooking crane by the hearth for the first fire. Both rituals are, of course, romantic excuses for a party, and this house is now amenable to celebrations of all varieties.

*T*he parlor has its share of painted finishes (*above*). A grain-painted chest, originally used to store blankets, serves as an end table to the wing chair. An antique pedestal table retains its original diamond-painted motif, a design echoed in the diamonds painted on the wide floor boards.

*T*elling details reflect the fresh approach to decorating shared by the owners. The cat portrayed by an anonymous folk artist (*opposite, clockwise from top left*) presides over a mantel. Lunch is a colorful affair with the addition of zinnias, anemones and cosmos in pewter pitchers. A collection of treens, or painted wood buckets, shares window space along with an herb topiary. The original door and iron hardware are back in service. A curious cabinet with scalloped edges is both an unusual storage case and perch for a contemporary decoy.

*D*ecorative woodwork and aged brick help give the "soul of an antique" to the ornamented mantel in the parlor (*top*). Furnishings don't necessarily match the period of the house. For example, the camelback sofa, bought secondhand, is vintage 1920s, and the Windsor chair happens to be a reproduction. However, the furnishings complement this "new-old" home beautifully.

The Federal Style popularized in London by architect Robert Adam, has a delicacy about it, while American interpretations (from 1790 to 1820) have a particular dignity. The stairway (*bottom*), with its symmetrical carving, reflects the original finesse of this style.

Authenticity in the preservation of the house was paramount to the owners, but they did take liberties when it came to decorating. It was not their intent to live in a museum, but rather to enjoy history with a degree of nonchalance. To wit, an architectural fragment rather than a conventional painting hangs over the sofa (*opposite*). The modern rolled-arm sofa is flanked by a primitive table on one side and a grain-painted trunk on the other.

Homer, Henry and Daisy are
regular guests in this bedroom
(*opposite*). What with the background
of textiles and folk art favored by
their family, the cats lead a
colorful life. The coverlet is an
unusual find from Pennsylvania.
Striped cotton runners (*above*) are
typical floor coverings in early
country houses and fit nicely in
this hallway. Another reminder
of the past is the wooden peg rack
that was the Shakers' simple answer
to a closet.

NEW FRONTIER

For those who choose the wilderness as their brand of escape, living styles lean to the casual. The home is an adventure, with energy coming from the possessions and, of course, the terrain.

This house radiates with the vigor of ski enthusiasts. Built halfway up Colorado's Snowmass Mountain, it is a shelter for the bold, self-reliant type and seems simultaneously to invite and defy the elements. The decorating style is appropriately graphic with an all-American theme, lumberjack colors and accents on sport.

Respectful of its site, the house is as subtle on the outside as it is exciting when you walk inside; it hardly intrudes on the mountain (*above*).

The living room (*opposite*) has a stone fireplace worthy of a rustic lodge, with its recessed bin for stockpiling logs. An Old Glory hooked rug stretched on a wooden frame establishes a patriotic theme in the house. The sofa is upholstered with blanket wool and the pillows are made of old Pendleton plaids. Hickory and rush chairs hold pillows covered in hunter's tartan, a motif quietly repeated in the wallpaper. A nailhead-trimmed trunk is ideal as a coffee table.

*T*he family room (*left*), vivid as a checkerboard, exudes a fun-and-games atmosphere. A vintage travel poster hangs on the jet-black wall adjacent to a graphically bold quilt hung over the sofa. Fragments of quilts cover the pillows, while checkered wool blankets serve as upholstery material. An old gameboard is at the ready—in this case as a snack tray. In the good-natured spirit of the room, a sleigh acts as an easy chair.

A tapestry of Americana (*opposite, clockwise from right*): the nostalgic sleigh with gleaming hardware and sumptuous black leather stationed in the family room; pillows covered in Indian-patterned blankets; a chair made of hickory branches and rush made warmer with blanket-plaid cushions; red and white graphics, from quilt pillows to windowpane-checkered sofa; windowseat corner of the bedroom; a detail of the quilt hanging; an inviting lounge chair festooned with pillows and a vibrant quilt.

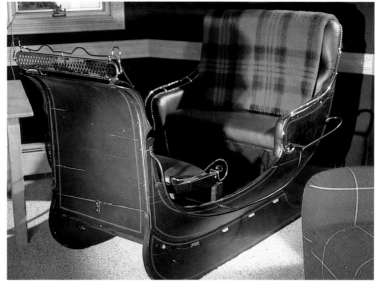

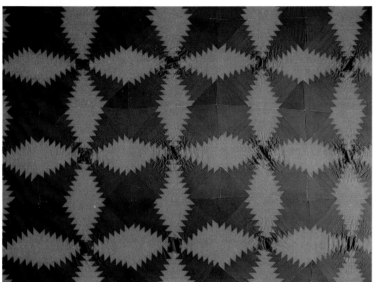

MODERN AND MELLOW

The dirt road led to a wooden bridge and lazy stream. On a summer day you could picnic here by a forest of white birch and honeysuckle. A breathtaking two-dozen acres of Connecticut country-side plus waterfall qualified as a miracle to the city couple who purchased the property. It was breathtaking.

What kind of house could measure up to such powerful landscape? To borrow from Walt Whitman: "When the materials are all prepared and ready, the architects shall appear. . . . I swear to you they will understand you and justify you. The greatest among them shall be he who best knows you. . . ." And so began a collaboration with architect Charles Gwathmey whose work the couple first started to admire in the sixties. Newlyweds

Angled toward the waterfall, the house communes with nature (*opposite*). Its primary materials, cedar walls and mahogany trim, have a rich warmth about them; staining the exterior every three years preserves the mellow patina. The living room's exposure to the hills is two-and-a-half stories high. Transparent as the house appears, it succeeds in feeling private and sheltered—a tribute to Gwathmey, who refers to it as "very soft and forgiving." The

owners' appreciation extends to the skeleton and round brick foundation that they consider as beautiful as the finished house.

The use of glass blocks at the entrance (*above*) filters light and allows a discreet connection with the outside. A small adjacent window captures a clear view. The door, reminiscent of a shoji screen, permits no view other than of itself—satisfaction enough.

*T*he dining area (*preceding page, left*) is like a terrazzo, its floor paved with slate and its view expansive. Exquisitely crafted mahogany cabinets and marble planes extend from the kitchen, a logical flow for entertaining. The table is actually a marble peninsula anchored to an arch between the cabinetry that houses a collection of architect-designed dishes.

The living room (*preceding page, right*) celebrates the soft side of modern architecture with its curves and color. Rose leather sofas are in the plush style of Robert Venturi, another influential architect. The green-glass coffee table is a Gwathmey-Siegel design.

A feat of cabinetry magic, the media unit (*opposite top, left*) is the flip side of the living room fireplace. This sitting area is of a more private nature, with a lowered ceiling and leather club chairs to curl up in (and watch old Fred Astaire movies all weekend). Smoked glass and clear panes create an oriental aura in this landing (*opposite top, right*), which houses laundry facilities behind the sliding mahogany-grid door.

Up a level from the entrance is the master bedroom suite (*opposite bottom, left*), a treetop domain. Its triangular fireplace relates to that in the living room below. Clad in cedar with mahogany floors and woodwork, the room is a deluxe cabin minus extraneous details. Not that it's without pleasure. Viewing TV in bed is

a matter of switching the remote control; the set rises on a hydraulic lift from the console at the foot. Curved ends hold speakers.

The adjoining bath (*opposite bottom, right*) spares no amenities. Double sinks are set into mahogany cabinets with green marble paving the counters and floor (easy to maintain, claims the owner). A separate room conceals toilet and bidet. The shower, housed in a windowed cylinder, is capped with a skylight.

The recreation area (*above*), situated off the guest wing, is an aesthetic composition of blue slate and flagstone. Bathers have a choice of two levels from which to gaze at the pool, whose midnight color and waved shape give it an organic quality.

then, they spent weekends in the Hamptons, where they formed lasting impressions of Gwathmey houses and an affection for the architect himself. In fact, it was the quality of endurance that struck the owners most about his work.

Not the aimless sort of dreamers, the couple set objectives for themselves. Even with the house's finesse, they talk about it as a work in progress. Within the next five years they plan to have the screened porch furnished so they can toast the sundown from that vantage point. Likely they'll build a sports compound with tennis court and pavilion near the pool. And they're now plotting a rock garden by the waterfall.

A Sense of History

•

Chez Givenchy

•

Plain and Fancy

•

In the French Manor

CHAPTER SIX

COUNTRY LUXE

One man's castle is another man's cottage. That is to say, a weekend house can be grand or humble. There is a common thread, however, that ties the two: a desire for comfort, intimacy and graciousness.

Whether a house is born with a pedigree or not, its quality of weekend life can be the same. One might have monogramed linens, another fresh flowers in every room, or boots and walking sticks at the front door for guests who have left theirs behind.

The owner is choreographer: responsible for planning, the condition of guest rooms, mix of guests, arrangement of activities or absence of same. One new summer-home owner tells of her query to guests at the end of weekend. What did they like the most is the question put forth in her guest book (a gracious way of recording weekend visitors and their comments). Sleeping on antique linens was the most enthusiastic reply, followed by the fresh scones set out for Sunday breakfast. She now has her eye out for old linens whenever shopping at country fairs. As for the scones, she's preparing recipe cards to set next to the basket so that guests can have a souvenir of the breakfast.

The most memorable weekend houses are those in which meals are celebrated. Even if it's Friday night pasta with fresh vegetables or a Saturday picnic basket for spreading out on the lawn, the thoughtfulness is a vital ingredient. Organizing such meals can be part of the work week's more pleasant activities. And if the weekend stretches to three days, all the better.

Joie de vivre is the point, whether the house in question is a French château or a New England farmhouse.

A SENSE OF HISTORY

W hat we aimed for here," says builder George Schneider, "was the characteristic Connecticut quality of warmth and informality, based loosely on English traditions. You might think of our inspiration as the stable on a large estate as it has been modified into living quarters over the centuries." Together with craftsman Bjorn Robinson Rye, he created this country-inn-style house along the path of a stream.

T he house (*above*) appears to have grown over time. The builders, no slaves to any particular style, have borrowed from the Georgians columns and fanlight windows. Local farms inspired the drive-through passage, clocktower and cupola. The profile is animated with gables, towers and dormers, all symbols of rural life.

T he entrance hall (*opposite*) nods to Georgian houses with marble floors, although this is a fanciful variation since its planks are painted. The craftsman-in-residence also applied his skills to the console table whose "marble" columns he painted. Its mirrored lower shelf creates an illusion of additional floor. The large pine-framed mirror provides its own reflections, giving the area a great feeling of spaciousness.

The English traditions built into this house are most evident in a conservatory dining room (*above*). Spires of delphinium catch the sun in a transparent room built with standard insulated glass. Its floor is white tile laid in brick fashion. A striped pine trestle table and natural wicker chairs have a year-round tropical feeling; colored terra-cotta plates add a zesty background for fruits and salads.

With its two sets of French doors leading to a balcony, the white-beamed living room (*opposite, top*) is outdoor oriented. An imposing masonry fireplace is also French in origin. The cupboard, one of a pair stationed between the fanlight-topped doors, was made by the designers of the house. It's filled with white ironstone; pitchers from the collection line the fireplace mantel.

The buttery shade of this room (*opposite, bottom*) is uplifting, with bowls of fruit and floral cushions emphasizing the good-natured ambience.

I HATH NOTHING UNDER

Budget was kept in control with the use of stock materials such as the kitchen cabinets (*opposite*) and columns. However, the decorations give the house a one-of-a-kind personality. How many kitchens would have a handpainted frieze exhorting you to eat, drink and be merry? The generations-old illusion is most convincing in the library (*top* and *above*), which is cozy with low beamed-ceiling and mellow woods. In reality, the mantel is newly made of stock moldings finished in a fruitwood stain that was not stirred, in order to achieve a light hue. Convincing, also, is the wall of books—actually a painted facsimile. Rolled-arm love seats offer intimate seating in a generous way.

CHEZ GIVENCHY

A weekend house by any other name could be called a *manoir*, that is, if it were located in France, as this is. An hour-and-a-half drive from Paris takes one to the Loire Valley and *Le Manoir du Jonchet*, the weekend home of fashion designer Hubert de Givenchy. Both regal looking, the house and its owner each have an informal side. As one guest recalls: "Within the thick stone walls of this centuries-old building, Hubert has created a setting of luxurious comfort and charmed elegance, totally free of the pomposity sometimes associated with château life."

Le Jonchet was built according to the fashions of the period from Henri IV to Louis XIII, which gives it a historical pedigree of awesome proportions; however,

A medieval-looking stairway (*above*) is graced with the skeleton of a lantern made by Diego Giacometti. Because the celebrated artist died before casting the lantern in bronze, M. de Givenchy has hung this plaster maquette as a tribute.

One of *Le Manior du Jonchet* towers (*opposite*) serves as a guest pavilion.

the classic lines and absence of ornamentation make it a felicitious place. The backyard may be larger than the norm (thirty acres), but the host sees to it that each guest has boots for hiking, not to mention every weekend comfort imaginable. Tea is set out in the salon off the stone-floored entry hall. The tray very likely holds homemade preserves and pastries and is placed on a glass-topped table between stacks of international magazines and books (new ones are provided each week). "In the country," says M. de Givenchy, "it is very important to have plenty of books, pillows and blankets." What sets this country house apart is that the pillows and blankets will be embroidered with the sign of *Le Jonchet*, for *jonc*, a marine plant similar to rush or cane.

*T*he salon (*opposite*) is dressed for summer with easy-fitting slipcovers and loose columns of white curtains made from Himalayan cotton, a fabric M. de Givenchy likes for more reasons than beauty. It is machine washable, a practical consideration for any house where two large dogs are welcome to curl up with guests. Tea is served here, on the glass table where there is always a fresh bouquet of white flowers.

A spaniel depicted in oil above a gilded writing desk (*left*) reflects the spirit of a gentleman's retreat deep in the heart of hunt country.

The entry hall (*right*) is outfitted with walking sticks, boots and all manner of country gear for guests to borrow.

The family tradition of using the same fabric for curtains, walls, chairs, bedhangings and pillows is carried on in the floral-covered bedroom (*opposite*). The designer says, "My mother and my aunt always decorated their bedrooms this way."

M. de Givenchy's love of fabrics is especially evident in the bedrooms. For an intimate, traditional look (*above*), fabric is gathered in hangings around the bed in richly upholstered chairs and headboard.

PLAIN AND FANCY

The humble cottage is just about the most versatile house of all. While simplicity is the prescribed decoration, there's nothing to stop a creative soul from taking a flight of fancy. Who better qualified than a design professional? J. Crawford, for example. He's the man responsible for much of Bonwit Teller's chic design and the founder of Quadrille, a textile and wallpaper firm.

The brick-paved terrace (*above*) exudes a definite English air with its garden bench and pots of daisies and hibiscus. A container garden such as this is gratifying for the weekend green thumb; it doesn't require the attention of, say, a mixed border or an in-ground garden. The pots can be moved about to accommodate entertaining, or easily replanted for summer variations with herbs and colorful annuals.

Homage to animals (*opposite*) gives special character to this small guest room. The painted iron bed is but one of the sources of interest. The original windows are festooned with cabbage-rose curtains, a motif featured in the rug, while the red wall, tempered by a white ceiling, holds the diversity of patterns together.

The house has grown over the years and several quirky additions are evidence of its unplanned expansion. Odd corners and crannies and unusual-shaped rooms are a plus for Crawford, who does not believe in housewide decorating schemes and who enjoys the individuality the architecture inspires.

"Being a painter and designer," says Crawford, "does free me from the idea that there are rules about color and style." This designer has no qualms about painting a ceiling Chinese red or gilding the crown molding above the windows in his dining room as "a way to entertain the eye." As a result, this classic shingle cottage, located on the South Shore of Long Island, New York, has come a long way from its plain beginnings in the nineteenth century.

The entrance (*above*) is the first clue that this is no plain-and-simple cottage. Having taken as many liberties as he saw fit, the owner created a tapestry with large Delft jars on black and gold Italianate brackets, rose chintzes and a Bessarabian rug. The windows, however, are basically unadorned, as is the heating pipe, both honest vestiges of the original cottage.

A Chinese-red ceiling (*opposite, top*) casts a warm glow on the dining room, a 1920s addition that was larger than the snug cottage required. The room is therefore decorated for intimacy with a high-backed sofa and circular table, but retains some aristocratic bearing with its wallpaper, a reproduction of one used in the king's bedroom at the Royal Pavilion in Brighton.

A sideboard (*opposite, bottom*) laden with fruits and vegetables also boasts a pair of blue ducks, placed there because, as their owner quips, "the color doesn't fit."

*U*npredictable decorating reaches upstairs to one of the guest bedrooms in the eaves (*top*). An antique Wild Goose Chase quilt might be pattern enough for most rooms, but the owner creates his own rhythm, covering walls and ceiling with more pattern of almost equal energy. "Strangeness is the unifying force," says Crawford of the unlikely combinations.

A Biedermeier desk is one of this room's elegant accoutrements (*bottom*). What could have been a naked corner next to it is embellished with a folding screen.

Another guest bedroom (*opposite*) has its share of antiques; the chair with rams' heads carved on its arms is nineteenth-century Italian; the black-lacquered mirror is English Regency and the black table, eighteenth-century Portuguese. Consistent with the black color scheme are a pair of electrified glass lamps converted from the original oil.

IN THE FRENCH MANOR

Getting away from it all on weekends can mean leaving one century for another. A three-hour drive from Paris, for example, transports you to the sixteenth century and a country house that denies any association with modern times, which is precisely what the family in residence intended. As members of the *Vieilles Maisons Françaises*, they are friends of old French houses and committed to authentic preservation of their own. Research told of this house's Norman influence, specifically with regard to the moat that forms a horseshoe around the house itself. However, the major part of the house was built in the eighteenth century and saved in this century by an intrepid group of relatives who set up dormitories in the attic and executed much of the restoration themselves (repairs to

A moat, attributed to the sixteenth-century Normans, is the manor's watering hole (*opposite*). An ivy-covered wing proves to be a good cushion for the stand-up reader, one of the family's four daughters. Geraniums in weathered pots are the only flowers on the terrace, a nonchalant place with grass allowed to push through cracks and vines given run of the walls. This offhand style extends to the unmatched terrace furniture. Wild roses turn a brick-arched door into a romantic ruin (*above*).

the roof, refacing the stucco). The decorative style is influenced by eighteenth-century styles, with provincial antiques mingling with those of richer backgrounds.

The work accomplished is one family's legacy and strong connection with the past. The concept of preserving historic French architecture is the purpose of an American sister organization called Friends of VMF. Incidentally, it offers members trips to culturally important French structures.

*T*ypical French esprit permeates the living room (*above, left*), whose walls and floors are jovial with pattern. Two-hundred-year-old ceiling timbers, hearth and wood paneling are complemented by two eighteenth-century love seats. One armchair wears a loose-fitting white slipcover, customary dress for summer in France. A wicker chaise is not out of place despite the relative formality of the room. It is a leisurely gesture that reflects both the personal character of the house and its nonconformist family. The dining room (*above, right*) departs from continuous pattern; its walls, finished with ocher-colored lime, have a medieval quality.

A brick-paved corridor seems to lead into another century (*opposite, top*). The primitive bench shares a wall with an early landscape painting that has the quality of an aged tapestry.

The tea service (*opposite, bottom*) blending into the wallpaper and the cotton fabric draped underneath the tray create a medley of patterns.

An herb-store cupboard (*below*) serves as a sort of kitchen file cabinet, evoking the domesticity of another era. A shallow armoire, (*top*) rising just shy of a beam, is used as a shelf for crockery.

A sink (*opposite, top, left*) is the kitchen's original sandstone relic, in which dishes are still washed the old-fashioned way by dipping them into a wooden bucket. The oak shelves are a modern efficiency, and an old English pine chest sits in a corner where the dinner's fruit and cheese course is prepared.

Forerunners of the modern laundry room: A room set aside for ironing (*opposite, top, right*) is one of the oldest in the manor, evidenced by its fireplace and stone floor. The ubiquitous checkered tablecloth matches the insert in an armoire, another staple of any French house. In another room (*opposite, bottom, left*) herbs are crushed with an antique mortar and pestle, then stored in the labeled cupboard. Sewing is aided by the light of a window (*opposite, bottom, right*) and with the help of somewhat modern machinery, the only visible vestige of this century.

*T*he guest bedroom, replete with breakfast table, exudes a warm-as-toast atmosphere (*above*). A faded quilt tablecloth and one winged chair add a dignified air. Particularly soothing are the room's hazelnut tans, unified with wallcovering and curtains. Improvisation, which the French do so well, is apparent in a wicker trunk topped by a pillow—voilà, a window seat.

A claw-foot tub has been reconstituted for weekend baths (*opposite*); its environment is still old world with hand-embroidered towels and half curtains. A wicker trunk serves as both hamper and tubside table. Instead of being relegated to back-of-door hooks, robes are hung conveniently near the bather.

First the Flowers

•

Weekends al Fresco

•

Homage to the Garden

•

Back to Nature

•

A Family Affair

CHAPTER SEVEN

WEEKEND GARDENS

Gardening is a passion that, when condensed to weekends, becomes all-consuming. No sooner does the car pull up to the weekend house than the weekend gardener lunges for the new growth of weeds, checks the soil for moisture and eyes the delphiniums to see if they are as upright as they were last Sunday. Dinner can wait; the garden gets priority.

The cycle of nature stops for no one, and so we must keep in step or suffer the consequences. "A garden is a taxing mistress," is the refrain of one country-house owner who cultivates the land with the help of her husband. Tasks that would normally be spread throughout the week must be accomplished on the weekend, demanding double time and supreme organization on the part of the gardener.

Weekend gardening is actually a year-round occupation, with the goal being an extended blooming season. Perennials give the garden its longevity and consistent shape, while annuals add color and variety. If the act of gardening becomes too overwhelming to be pleasurable,

there are shortcuts, like the container garden where perennials, annuals and vegetables can be grown in terra-cotta pots arranged on decks, terraces or grass.

Gardens, whether in a small cluster of pots or a grand layout of mixed borders, are artistic expressions. For many houses, the garden is the focus of activity, from planting to pruning, from cutting flowers to gathering produce for summer meals. The process is ongoing and demanding. Then suddenly it's October and hedges must be pruned, compost heaps built, leaves raked. Come November, the lawn may need lime, evergreens water and the flowers drying. It's all in a weekend's work, for the gardener lets no grass grow under his feet.

One of America's most enthusiastic gardeners, Thomas Jefferson, left a profound mark on his beloved Monticello. His gardens bring an awareness of early plant species, and are a source of inspiration for anyone who believes as Jefferson did, that "no occupation is so delightful as the culture of the earth, and no culture comparable to that of the garden."

FIRST THE FLOWERS

"To own a bit of ground, to scratch it with a hoe, to plant seeds and watch the renewal of life— this is the commonest delight of the race, the most satisfactory thing a man can do." The sentiment of Charles Dudley Warner is certainly as applicable to-day as it was in 1870, when he wrote "My Summer in a Garden." The fervor for gardening, in fact, is turning record numbers of seed-catalog readers into landscape artists and timid planters into risk takers. Satisfaction is at the root of it all.

The owners of this property took to the garden before doing anything much to their nineteenth-century Con-necticut barn. "We reclaimed the land," says the couple

A monumental rhododendron (*opposite*) drops its petals on a silvery garden bench; both have developed more character with age.

A view of the house from a fence (*top*) built by the owner. A trip to England's Cotswolds inspired his rendition of the lyrical fence in which euonymus and white clematis entwine themselves.

Lattice is well suited to the climbing habits of clematis (*bottom*), a beautifully tough climber. This is a particularly robust variety with flowers the size of a large hand.

of the garden, which, although neglected, had dozens of peonies and a remarkable cascading rhododendron. Theirs was an ambitious venture that involved hauling stones, widening herbaceous borders and employing the tedious soil-enrichment method called double digging, or feeding the soil two spades deep. However, the process has been spaced out over many years, and like all inveterate gardeners, this couple is still experimenting and heeding advice of old sages like England's Vita Sackville-West. "Hoick it out," was her simple solution for plants that didn't provide the satisfaction expected.

Devotion to gardening spills into the barn's living room (*above*) with English floral chintz and (*opposite*) ceramics designed in a stunning vegetable motif. Sisal matting covers the floor in a natural texture that corresponds with the pale wood interior. A ficus tree seems to be edging its way to the rafters, where light is also plentiful. French doors were additions to a room where plans for a greenhouse are shaping up.

A mixed border (*top, left*) features white iris in the foreground. Well-cultured peonies (*top, right*) are a vibrant contrast to the native-stone wall.

A pathway of fieldstone (*bottom, right*) wears moss that spreads with abandon. The moss was coin-size when transplanted from a friend's garden. Siberian irises called 'Dreaming Spires' (*bottom, left*) are sources of brilliant color in the garden and for bouquets.

The towering rhododendron (*opposite*) nearly obscures an outbuilding; it is the flourish at the end of a serpentine border with peonies in top form.

WEEKENDS AL FRESCO

T axing as a garden can be, its rewards are worth every hour of toil. If two share the workload, Monday morning aches and pains are lessened while productivity doubles. Joy and Robert K. Lewis head for the garden immediately upon reaching their weekend cottage on Long Island. For the Lewises, the garden is the hub of all activity throughout the summer. The fruits of their labors include a formal herb garden with charming brick paths, a very efficient shed, an apple orchard that yields antique varieties, a wildflower garden and a grape arbor. Their most recent project was of a practical nature; they installed sprinkler hoses on timers so that the mixed borders can be tended-to by remote control. For Robert Lewis, a busy interior designer, time-saving techniques are crucial, yet he never shuns the basics of classic gardening, taught to him by his grandmother when he was five years old.

W isteria vines wrap around the top of the front porch on the Lewises' 1830s house (*above*). Traditional boxwood, hollyhocks and delphiniums, and baskets of vegetables picked for that day's dinner, give the house a "lived-in" and loved quality. That feeling is evident in a view of the garden from the terrace (*opposite*).

The immaculate lawn and perennial borders (*opposite, top*) set the scene for summer entertaining, be it happy parties or warm family breakfasts. The perspective is lengthened by a garden bench whose origin, like the garden style, is English.

A walk through the Lewis garden is certain to yield lavender (*opposite, left and right*), which Mr. Lewis grows in abundance. Guests are often treated to bouquets, spontaneously put together on such walks. When strawberries are in season, they often accompany fragrant bouquets of honeysuckle, lemon verbena and peppermint-scented geranium leaves gathered on this work table.

A surplus of flowers (*above*) is the reward for all that weeding, mulching and care.

HOMAGE TO
THE GARDEN

The most imaginative houses usually belong to those with an artistic streak. Robert Jackson certainly qualifies; he's often commissioned to paint murals for private houses or to execute decorative arts projects like the Gothic Revival Library at the Metropolitan Museum of Art in New York City. Like the fireman on holiday, Jackson continues painting on his weekends in the country, a Hudson River Valley location. What's more, his fascination with Gothic arches and painted effects spills over from his professional artistry. There is a definite Gothic mood about his 1900s farmhouse, some of it architectural and some created by his brush.

Old frames (*opposite*) collected with no particular purpose in mind become part of a bigger still life arranged on a well-worn cupboard. Natural light pours in from a series of windows—a picturesque background. Jackson added a porch (*above*), inspired by those in the neighboring Hudson River Valley, with trim taken from here and there. The amusing columns are almost obscured by Virginia creeper, a vine that threatens to invade the house if not clipped regularly. Gothic arches announce the owner's interest in that decorative period.

Jackson takes the paintbrush where the spirit moves him, which turns out to be any surface in the house, including the floor. That artistic streak is not contained indoors. His garden is one composition after another, with flowers inspiring Jackson to paint more. His relationship with nature, therefore, is quid pro quo; what the ground produces, he reproduces—on canvas or possibly a wall.

The living room (*opposite, top*) has a blush about it, with the help of rosy-beige walls. Its decorative molding was applied with paint, as was the "stone" floor.

Jackson has the agility of a magician when he takes paintbrush in hand. The Gothic arches on the mantel (*opposite, bottom*), believe it or not, aren't carved; they are painted with fool-the-eye techniques mastered by the owner. Three pitchers of roses, in this setting, get double exposure against a mirror; ditto for a pair of candles. The reflection also includes one of Jackson's cloud paintings.

The dining room (*above*) is an artistic tour de force, its mural a folk-style depiction of the surrounding Hudson River Valley. The floors, too, are handpainted, actually with a sponge dabbed in black and applied to the dark green floor. This was Jackson's remedy for floors in need of improvement.

*R*obert Jackson (*top*) re-creates a foxglove on canvas, an homage to his garden.

*T*he entrance of this house (*bottom*) features arched windows capped with diamonds painted by the artist to continue his favorite Gothic theme.

*T*he entry hall (*opposite*) is a veritable nature walk with a life-size iris created by the owner. A twig basket and bark birdhouse accompany fresh-picked flowers likely to become the subject of a painting. The folded ribbon molding is one of the many painted effects executed by the artist-in-residence.

Gardening plays a dual role in Jackson's weekend life. It's both the result of his artistic instincts and a source of subject matter for his painting. The floral palette (*above*) leans to the soft colors he favors on canvas. Flower beds are arranged with a keen eye for scale and mass: peonies balanced by foxglove on the opposite border; an old finial that once topped a gatepost ornaments an open area between hemlock hedges. As

they continue to mature, the hedges will become greater walls for this outdoor room.

Now divided into pathways and private areas, the garden is a series of visual surprises. Along the way, visitors come upon a patch of old-fashioned roses (*opposite, top*). One path from the rear of the house (*opposite, bottom*) leads to a galaxy of perennials graduated in height.

BACK TO NATURE

A gathering of roses, cosmos, baby's breath and other garden cuttings (*opposite*) awaits drying and experimentation as a potpourri.

Originally the carriage house of one of the oldest horse farms in America, this home was found through an advertisement in an antiques journal. The owners added a wraparound porch appropriate to the stone-and-shingle cottage (*above*).

A calm environment is what most hard-working people crave, yet many have been known to knock themselves out in the pursuit. Calm, after all, takes practice; it's as much a state of mind as condition of home. One daily practitioner is Barbara Ohrbach, whose weekend house reflects cultivation, and, as a result, serenity.

A carriage house in New York State is a source of renewal for a woman who makes quality of life a profession. Author of several best-selling style books and owner of Cherchez, a boutique she and her husband founded, Ohrbach is as earnest about her weekend life as she is about her work. Both are the sum of creative endeavors including gardening and collecting. Therefore the country pace is energetic, what with seedlings to be started, flowers to be dried and potpourri mixed for her business. When not in the garden, chances are she'll be working on some other project or moving furniture around to make room for an antique she couldn't live without.

*N*ieces and nephews join Barbara Ohrbach in a summer weekend custom: sorting out flowers for drying. A towel rack holds bunches of lavender and other flowers tied with rubber bands (*above, left and right*).

*B*askets serve to collect flowers and decorate the kitchen (*opposite, top*). An old apple sink holds dried flowers. The shelf, made from the decorative wood of a window valance, displays blue-and-white Staffordshire china. Vintage linoleum was retained as a floor covering, a once-popular style that's enjoying a comeback.

*R*ounded clay pots reminiscent of southern France hold herbs (*opposite, bottom, left*). An antique plant stand and watering cans are fruits of many travels. White deck enamel unifies the porch with the railing.

Unmatched chairs surround the dining table (*bottom, right*) and a Mexican shawl serves as a runner. The blue and white color scheme is vividly established with a quilt wall hanging.

The living room (*opposite, top*) harks back to old sun porches with its wicker and twig rockers. Pinecones and dried lavender sit in a wooden box under a salvaged mantelpiece. With little wall space above the mantel, miniature antique prints were chosen for decorations.

More evidence of Barbara's infatuation with flora (*opposite, bottom, left*): a rustic half-moon table holds dried rose petals; garden books flank a weathered urn filled with enough dried lavender to scent the room.

Here, a setting speaks of individuality (*opposite, bottom, center*): a Victorian quilt rests behind a needlepoint pillow, the handwork of Mr. Ohrbach; needlepoint footstools sit next to a trunk holding a collection of 1920s ceramic boxes.

An eave (*opposite, bottom, right*) allows for other romantic opportunities. A circular table covered with antique cloths serves as a photo gallery. In Victorian fashion, the lamp has a lace bonnet. A wicker lounge chair beckons the wearied weekender to curl up and read.

The bedroom (*above*) is a den of tranquillity and a haven for personal treasures. "On my travels," says Ms. Ohrbach, "I buy what I can't live without and then find a space for it." Consequently, things get moved about. As of this moment, a dressmaker's dummy stands under the eaves, an appropriate participant in a feminine scene.

A FAMILY AFFAIR

A second home is often the result of many other homes lived in or visited before. In other words, it can be a composite of ideas, a wish list satisfied. Suppose you are an inveterate keeper of scrapbooks who is given to clipping bits about gardens, porches, bedrooms and the like. Those ideas will have relevance someday.

Scrapbooks representing years of favorite country places funneled into this seaside cottage, built as a guesthouse for a family who simply couldn't all fit under one roof. After purchasing the main house a number of years ago, the owner began to visualize (from the closets out) this place for guests, specifically her twelve grandchildren and their parents. A large porch was one requisite, as was a double-height living room with a balcony. Logically, the house needed sufficient sleeping quarters; this was to be an endless vacation spot and the building of a family tradition. Indeed, the Shingle Style and surrounding porch are the elements we equate with continuity, with traditional summer homes of which scrapbooks are made.

Accentuated details (*above*) top the gray-shingled house designed by architect James Volney Righter. He used oversize dentils around the porch eaves with spaces in-between to vent the roof. The natural wood shingles, a seaside tradition, have an ornamental quality above the dormered windows where they sweep downwards in a graceful curve.

The surrounding porch (*opposite*) is somewhat like a boardwalk, with a sea of green lawn as its vista. The curved roof and columns add a certain grace and sense of age.

*T*he living room (*opposite*) capitalizes on an enviable view of a wandering creek and natural-style gardens. Its double height allows for separate areas of congregation—on the first level off the porch or on the balcony fitted with a sofa. Either way, the view is widespread. To help control the flood of sunlight, lower bay windows have fabric blinds held taut and nearly invisible when not in use. Uppermost windows vent out hot air.

The stair landing is also an eave; therefore it has been captured as an intimate nook for writing and reading (*right, top*). A banquette built under the windows makes efficient use of a tight space.

Beds are arranged foot to foot so that the arched window is given full sweep (*right, below*). This arrangement inspires visiting grandchildren to flop on the long stretch of beds as if they were one giant sofa. The upholstered headboards repeat the shape of the window, whose breeze precludes the need for air-conditioning.

Among the owner's bits in her scrapbook were pictures of gardens and their sundry ornaments. A fancier of the English garden—its gazebos, lattice and mixed borders—she integrated all of the most admired elements into this property.

The lacy gazebo, picket fence and arch (*above*) form points of interest in the garden and give it the quality of an outdoor room. Here there is a steady supply of color and cutting flowers, what with the profusion of white cleome, pink cosmos, mauve ageratum and white veronica.

Obviously well planned, garden areas (*opposite*) were created from fields, with flowers planted in drifts as the English are known to do. No instant garden, this; it evolved as the land became more familiar to its owner. One boggy spot, a particular challenge, is now a lily pond with ornamental grasses swaying at its bank.

Copyright, pages 4–5, William P. Steele

Contents, page 6 (clockwise from top left), Tom Yee, Michael Skott, Christopher Ivion, Michael Skott; page 7 (clockwise from top left), Jeff McNamara, Langdon Clay, Kari Haavisto, Michael Skott.

Introduction, pages 8–11 , Kari Haavisto

COTTAGES

American Cotswold, pages 14–19, Lilo Raymond;
Small Wonder, pages 20–25, Michael Skott;
Cottage-Style Decorating, pages 26–29, Michael Skott;
Cheerful Thirties Cottage, pages 30–35, Lilo Raymond;
Tasteful Simplicity, pages 36–41, Joshua Greene;
Gamekeeper's Cottage, pages 42–45, Michael Dunne.

FARMHOUSES

Forgotten Farmhouse, pages 48–53, Joshua Greene;
Blending Three Barns, pages 54–61, Norman McGrath;
A Gentleman's Farm, pages 62–69, Kari Haavisto;
Farmhouse Modern, pages 70–73, Langdon Clay;
Vintage Napa, pages 74–79, Christopher Ivion.

GREAT ESCAPES

Taking In the View, pages 82–85, Norman McGrath;
Double Identity, pages 86–89, Tom Yee;
View from the Veranda, pages 90–97, William P. Steele;
New Slant on the Small House, pages 98–101, John Hall;
Mountain Home, pages 102–105, Elyse Lewin;
In the Western Spirit, pages 106–111, Tom Yee.

A HOUSE BY ANY OTHER NAME

The Mill, pages 114–119, Michael Skott;
Rustic Schoolhouse, pages 120–123, Jeff McNamara;
Little Blue Shed, pages 124–127, Joe Standart;
Chicken-Coop Cottage, pages 128, 129, 130 (*bottom*), Peter Bosch, pages 130 (*top*) and 131, Tom Yee.

PERSONAL VISION

All-American Country, pages 134–141, Michael Skott;
Imaginative Leap, pages 142–145, Tom Yee;
Remaking History, pages 146–153, Michael Skott;
New Frontier, pages 154–157, Jeff McNamara;
Modern and Mellow, pages 158–163, Langdon Clay.

COUNTRY LUXE

A Sense of History, pages 166–171, Langdon Clay;
Chez Givenchy, pages 172–177, Michael Dunne;
Plain and Fancy, pages 178–183, William P. Steele;
In the French Manor, pages 184–191, Michael Dunne.

WEEKEND GARDENS

First the Flowers, page 195 (*top*), William P. Steele, pages 194, 195 (*bottom*), 196-199, Lilo Raymond;
Weekends al Fresco, pages 200–203, Chris Callas;
Homage to the Garden, pages 204, 206, 207, 208 (*top*), 209, 210, 211 (*top*), Michael Skott, pages 205, 208 (*bottom*), 211 (*bottom*), Lilo Raymond;
Back to Nature, pages 212–217, Kari Haavisto;
A Family Affair, pages 218–223, Judith Watts Wilson.